'In this book Viv and Hele[...] tested Theraplay principles [...] help to increase the emotional health of our children. This book gives many ideas and clear structure to help all parents provide an emotionally rich and connected parenting environment.'

— *Kim Golding, consultant clinical psychologist and author of* Everyday Parenting with Security and Love

'This clear, concise, accessible and practical book will be welcomed by parents and carers of children with traumatic pasts. When family life has become a struggle, this book can show exhausted, demoralised parents the way back to having fun together, while repairing damage and building trust in their wounded child in the process. I highly recommend it as a resource for all adoptive parents to dip into when needed.'

— *Ann Bell, Director Wales/Cyfarwyddwr* *Cymru, Adoption UK*

'If you have had doubts or have forgotten about the importance of those magical times of relationship play with our children, here is a book by Viv Norris and Helen Rodwell, *Parenting with Theraplay*®, that will be the only reminder that you need. These ways of connecting with our children continuously strengthen our relationships with them and enable us to then guide and direct them within a context of trust, comfort and joy and with much less conflict. Understanding and bringing to life the many ideas contained in this book will be of great value to us and to our children.'

— *Daniel Hughes, Ph.D., Founder of* *Dyadic Developmental Psychotherapy*

'What a joy to read a book whose ideas based on slow parenting allow for the growth of children at a human pace. In an age when so much of what we appear to do with our children is focused on creating a product, the idea of parents feeling confident enough to trust that lending a hand to their children, by setting the pace with gentle help, brings with it a sigh of relief and joy. This is a tranquil book where the reader is led by the hand and yet the practical ideas and accessible knowledge gifted to the reader light up the brain like a Christmas tree.'

— *Veronica Read, Group Analyst and Educational Consultant and author of* Developing Attachment in Early Years Settings *and* Building Positive Relationships with Parents of Young Children

'Throughout my time as an adoptive parent to two developmentally traumatised children, I've always known that there has been a missing piece of the puzzle. *Parenting with Theraplay®* and the techniques so well described in it tackle those things I knew weren't right, but were so easily dismissed. If you have a child who chews the cuffs of their school sweatshirt until there are no cuffs left, or who struggles to engage with play, or who is always teetering on the edge of or jumping into hyper-arousal, or who battles you over everything, or who can't bear to be touched, or who hugs you so tightly you think your ribs might break, then buy this book right now. It is written in a helpful, kind and practical way and doesn't make you feel as though you need to be a super-parent 24/7. As the authors say, Theraplay is about giving hope and increasing joy and their book does that with bubbles, feathers and face paints on.'

— *Sally Donovan, author of* The Unofficial Guide to Adoptive Parenting *and* Billy Bramble and The Great Big Cook Off

Parenting
with Theraplay®

of related interest

Using Stories to Build Bridges with Traumatized Children
Creative Ideas for Therapy, Life Story Work, Direct Work and Parenting
Kim S. Golding
ISBN 978 1 84905 540 6
eISBN 978 0 85700 961 6

Everyday Parenting with Security and Love
Using PACE to Provide Foundations for Attachment
Kim S. Golding
Illustrated by Alex Barrett
Foreword by Dan Hughes
ISBN 978 1 78592 115 5
eISBN 978 1 78450 384 0

Attaching Through Love, Hugs and Play
Simple Strategies to Help Build Connections with Your Child
Deborah D. Gray
ISBN 978 1 84905 939 8
eISBN 978 0 85700 753 7

A Guide to Therapeutic Child Care
What You Need to Know to Create a Healing Home
Ruth Emond, Laura Steckley and Autumn Roesch-Marsh
ISBN 978 1 84905 401 0
eISBN 978 0 85700 769 8

Why Can't My Child Behave?
Empathic Parenting Strategies that Work for Adoptive and Foster Families
Dr Amber Elliott
ISBN 978 1 84905 339 6
eISBN 978 0 85700 671 4

Games and Activities for Attaching With Your Child
Deborah D. Gray and Megan Clarke
ISBN 978 1 84905 795 0
eISBN 978 1 78450 152 5

Parenting
with
Theraplay®

Understanding Attachment
and How to Nurture a Closer
Relationship with Your Child

Vivien Norris and Helen Rodwell

Forewords by **Phyllis Booth** and **Dafna Lender**
Illustrations by **Miranda Smith**

Jessica Kingsley *Publishers*
London and Philadelphia

First published in 2017
by Jessica Kingsley Publishers

www.jkp.com

Library of Congress Cataloging in Publication Data
Title: Parenting with Theraplay : understanding attachment and how to nurture
  a closer relationship with your child / Vivien Norris and Helen Rodwell.
Description: London ; Philadelphia : Jessica Kingsley Publishers, [2017]
Identifiers: LCCN 2017004826 (print) | LCCN 2017020999 (ebook) | ISBN
  9781784504892 (ebook) | ISBN 9781785922091 (alk. paper)
Subjects: LCSH: Parent and child. | Attachment behavior in children. | Play
  therapy.
Classification: LCC BF723.P25 (ebook) | LCC BF723.P25 N67 2017 (print) | DDC
  649/.1--dc23

British Library Cataloguing in Publication Data
A CIP catalogue record for this book is available from the British Library

ISBN 978 1 78592 209 1
eISBN 978 1 78450 489 2

Printed and bound in the United States

To my children Oscar, Oliver, Martha and Ben

Vivien Norris

*For my children Eloise and Andrew
and my adorable husband*

Helen Rodwell

also available from JKP

Theraplay The Practitioner's Guide

By Vivien Norris and Dafna Lender,
foreword by Phyllis Booth

£27.99 | $34.95 | PB | 392PP | ISBN 978 1 78592 210 7 |
eISBN 978 1 78450 488 5

Theraplay® – *The Practitioner's Guide* is an ideal introduction and overview for any professional working with children and families. This comprehensive guide outlines the theory, reflection and skill development of the practitioner – the true power house of Theraplay®.

Theraplay Theory, Applications and Implementation

Edited by Sandra Lindaman and Rana Hong, foreword by Phyllis Booth

£35.00 | $45.00 | PB | 288PP | ISBN 978 1 78775 070 8 |
eISBN 978 1 78775 071 5

Theraplay® – *Theory, Applications and Implementation* is a handbook providing concrete, practical assistance on deepening Theraplay knowledge and skills. From toddlers to adolescents and settings ranging from home schools, out-patient mental health, dyadic and group Theraplay and client issues such as interpersonal violence, LGBTQ families, anxiety, child sexual abuse, foster care and adoption, this book is essential for any Theraplay practitioner wanting to ensure their approach is fully informed and tailored to their client's needs.

Contents

Foreword

Phyllis Booth (Co-Founder of Theraplay)

I am delighted that Viv and Helen have written a book for parents based on the attachment-focused Theraplay model. The language is clear and simple, and the lively illustrations provide an easy-to-use guide that will help you create the vibrant, loving family we all dream of. In making the intuitive wisdom of Theraplay available to all parents, they bring Theraplay back to its roots in the model of natural, healthy parenting that creates family well-being.

To help you understand what I mean, I will briefly tell you about how Theraplay began in the United States Head Start programme. Recognising the needs of all children for early supportive and stimulating experiences, the US government initiated a nationwide programme designed to provide a 'Head Start' for three- and four-year-old children from low-income, high-risk families. As you might expect some of the children needed more than a good preschool programme. Ann Jernberg, creator of Theraplay, was given the job of finding a way to help these unsettled and needy children who were often upset and angry, or shut down and sad. She turned to the model of what parents naturally do with their babies and young children: play with them, take care of them, connect with them. I joined her eagerly in this effort to find ways to help these children.

My own childhood experiences gave me lots of good ideas. My mother was always ready to comfort and reassure me if I was unhappy. I remember lots of cuddles, and the comforting pleasure of holding hands with her. She responded with loving attention when I was unhappy or ill. When my sister and I came home from school on a rainy day, she would have hot cocoa ready and we would play games together on the living room floor.

My father's play was more boisterous. I remember many happy times when he lifted me up onto his knees as he lay on the floor: 'One for the money, Two for the show, Three to get ready' – pause – '*and four to go*!' The delicious excitement of anticipation, the moment of swooping down, the hug as I landed on his tummy! 'More! More!' I would shout.

But playing and cuddling wasn't the only thing we did in my family. There were chores to do, beds to be made, dishes to wash, food to cook, homework to be done. These were all done with an air of competent completion, spiced with a dash of playfulness. Making the beds together with my mother, I run ahead and hide under the sheets. Arriving at the rumpled bed, she playfully tries to smooth it, 'Oh, there's a lump in my bed!' I giggle as she attempts to smooth the lump out. 'What is it?' She finds my hair, 'Oh, it's a mop!' I pop out. 'Oh, it's Phyllis!' A good hug and then as an efficient, coordinated team, we smooth the bed making it fresh and inviting for the next night's cosy sleep.

With the model of healthy parenting in mind, Ann Jernberg and I gathered a team of playful, young mental health workers to spend time one-on-one with the children in the Head Start programme who needed help. Our goal was to give the children the caring, attuned and joyful experiences that all children deserve. To our delight the children began to feel better. Angry, acting-out children calmed down and were able to play and cooperate with their peers. Sad, shut down children became more outgoing and lively.

The essential healing power of the Theraplay approach is in the positive relationship that is created between the children and the adults who care for them. Since those early beginnings Theraplay has spread around the world as a therapeutic model that has helped thousands of families regain or achieve this happy state that promises so much for the development of healthy children.

In creating this book, with its many ideas for ways to connect with your children, Viv and Helen have brought the Theraplay ideas back to where they started – in the everyday interactions between you and your children. It is not just a book to read, it is a book to put into practice. You will learn many important things as you read the book, but you will experience the most important message as you put these playful, engaging and loving activities into action. The comfort and joy in your family will amply reward you.

Foreword

Dafna Lender (Programme Director,
The Theraplay® Institute)

When Vivien and Helen told us of their intent to write a parenting book based on Theraplay principles, we at The Theraplay® Institute in Evanston, IL, USA, let out a cry of joy and relief! Finally, a book on Theraplay written for parents that will explain the simple, essential and oft-forgotten parenting principles to help families thrive! For 50 years, The Theraplay® Institute has focused on training as many psychotherapists in the Theraplay method as possible so that they could help children heal. But what about the parents and children who don't need a visit to a therapist, but where joy and connection between them seemed to be overshadowed by the obligations and stresses of everyday life? Many families asked us to write a book to address these issues, but the leadership were too busy to undertake the task. Then along came Vivien and Helen. We could think of no better people to write this book for parents: Vivien Norris and Helen Rodwell are shining stars in the universe of parenting wisdom. They combine the highest calibre of professional rigour with personal experience and uncompromised compassion. Between them they have worked with hundreds of children and their families in the quest to find harmony and connection at home.

Rest assured that Theraplay is based on the most up-to-date scientific research on developmental psychology, neurobiology and trauma theory. Theraplay has also been rated as 'Effective' (highest rating) by the United States Department of Mental Health and Substance Abuse. Helen and Vivien have summarised the most relevant 'whys' and 'whats' of the method so that you can get to the heart of the matter as quickly as possible: how to feel more connected with your child so that you can have a cooperative and joyful family life.

Acknowledgements

Our aim in writing this book has been to present the Theraplay approach in a straightforward and accessible way so that busy parents will be able to quickly understand the approach and how it works in everyday life. We have deliberately tried to find a conversational tone and to present the book in a way which avoids jargon and detailed referencing. The risk is that we may have misrepresented some of the more complex ideas but we hope that the accessibility of this text outweighs any errors. We have of course been influenced by a wide range of authors, researchers and clinicians, and draw upon many different ideas. We would like to acknowledge the work of many leaders in the field and hope that you feel your work has been adequately represented: John Bowlby, Mary Ainsworth, Mary Main, Daniel Stern, Berry Brazleton, Colwyn Trevarthen, Ed Tronick, Paul MacLean, Mary Dozier, Jon Baylin, Sandra Bloom, Peter Fonagy, Stephen Porges, Allan Schore, Dan Siegel, Dan Hughes, Susan Hart, Pat Ogden, Jean Ayers, Eadaoin Bhreathnach and Tiffany Field.

Our understanding of Theraplay is constantly developing through our work with parents and children and through discussion with our colleagues. We are extremely grateful for their confidence and generosity. We received rich feedback on drafts from colleagues and parents, which undoubtedly improved the book. Thanks to

Phyllis Booth, Jodi Pennington, Josie Allen, Nic Jones, Jen Forsyth, Kim Golding, Dafna Lender, Sally Waters Foster, Mark Smith, Lisa Turton and Graham Street.

Miranda Smith has provided a range of delightful and engaging illustrations which are a lovely addition to this book. They bring a feeling of doing and experiencing Theraplay, which is what Theraplay is all about.

We very much appreciate the endorsement given to this project by our colleagues at The Theraplay® Institute who immediately supported the idea and have provided encouragement throughout. Dafna Lender has, over several years, developed the parent training programme for The Theraplay® Institute and we are very grateful for her openness and contribution to this book.

Most importantly we want to thank Phyllis Booth for her enthusiastic and very detailed feedback at each stage. The process of sending drafts and receiving Phyllis' comments has been a pleasure in itself, like having a wise parent who, as in Bowlby's famous line, 'is bigger, stronger, wiser and kind'. Without Phyllis and her late colleague Ann Jernberg there would be no Theraplay.

Introduction

Theraplay[1] is a practical approach for helping children and their families, which is active and playful and promotes closeness. It is an approach that can benefit all families. You might find you aren't enjoying life together and want a bit of help or perhaps something has happened (like a bereavement, illness or divorce) which has made things in your family feel less secure. You may have more significant difficulties or may be starting from scratch in trying to make a relationship with a fostered or adopted child, or perhaps you are a new step-parent. Whatever your situation, Theraplay can offer ideas for how to connect with your child and help you find ways to move forward together. This book will introduce you to the Theraplay approach and the main ideas that it is based on.

The book is divided into two main sections. The first part tells you what Theraplay is and the second part offers suggestions for handling everyday practical situations. The book is designed to give you as parents, carers and supporters some ideas about how you can use the Theraplay approach in everyday life to strengthen your family relationships. It is full of ideas and examples and, we hope, enough explanation to enable you to see why it

---

1   A registered service mark of The Theraplay® Institute, 1840 Oak Avenue Suite 320 Evanston, IL 60201.

can work. It may also be helpful as an introduction if you are involved in more specialist work with a professional.

Part 1: What Is Theraplay?

In the first six chapters, we talk about the basic building blocks of Theraplay: what it is, the main theoretical ideas that it is based on, and the four main themes (Structure, Engagement, Nurture and Challenge) that make up the Theraplay approach.

Part 2: Everyday Examples

In chapters seven to ten we think about everyday ways of using Theraplay ideas. We look at transitions and change and difficult behaviours, answer some common questions and describe lots of activities you can try.

Notes on terminology

Throughout the book the term 'parent' is used to describe the range of caregivers who provide an everyday parenting role for the children they are caring for.

We have alternated use of male and female pronouns by chapter.

We have described a wide range of activities throughout this book. We would like to acknowledge that the way in which families interact and play differs greatly across families and cultures. We are inevitably influenced by our own culture and would invite you to adapt the ideas to suit your own family and context.

Part 1

What Is Theraplay?

1

What Is Theraplay and How Does It Work?

Theraplay is a way for adults and children to be together which deepens the relationship between them. It centrally involves the parent in engaging in particular ways with their child. Theraplay draws on a wide range of very simple activities that create 'in the moment' connection between two people and develop closeness. The activities themselves are just a vehicle to help with this connection and, through the process of sensitive 'here and now' interaction, the child is able to relax and be a child. The activities are led by the adult and are varied, some lively, some quiet, and they require few or no materials.

The Theraplay approach developed out of a project in the 1960s in Chicago called the Head Start programme, which was designed to support children and families living in at-risk or deprived circumstances. The developers of Theraplay spent considerable time observing how typical parents and children interacted and came up with a range of playful activities that they thought could help children with difficulties. They quickly realised that it would be very important to include parents and carers in the play. They called this relationship-focused approach Theraplay.

The aim was to strengthen the relationship between the children and their carers. Using a range of simple play activities, they hoped to help children feel better about themselves and to reduce difficult behaviours. What surprised everyone working on the project was how much day-to-day problem behaviours improved, even without discussing them. Aggressive children became calmer, withdrawn children came out of their shell. Parents felt more confident and closer to their children. It seemed that supporting families to interact in a positive and relationship-focused way, through the play activities, was having a profound effect on all areas of family life.

In the years since the early success of Theraplay, there has been a lot of research by scientists, academics and practitioners who are interested in the kinds of parenting that lead to healthy development in children. We now have much more understanding about what is happening in the developing brain. Theraplay has benefited from this research and has been refined to become a focused therapy approach. There has been a great deal of thinking about the underlying theory and an increasing body of research about its effectiveness. Theraplay is now practised by various professionals across the world and with a range of groups from infants, children and parents to the elderly.

It is being delivered by practitioners in homes, specialist therapy centres and schools.

 The Theraplay approach began with a practical question: What can we do to help improve parent–child relationships which is simple, effective and long lasting? The answer: Theraplay.

Is Theraplay only used by professionals or can you use the ideas at home?

Theraplay can be used as an approach in many different ways and contexts. Some professionals are highly trained and experienced and will use Theraplay as a focused therapy approach – that is, as formal therapy provision. If your difficulties are complex you may need to seek trained help. There is more information about this in Chapter 9. In addition, there are many situations where the ideas can be useful without formal training. This book focuses on the everyday use of Theraplay ideas within your family.

Theraplay is based upon what ordinary successful parents do with their children. Parents typically provide safety and organisation, play and delight, nurture and care and they encourage their child (with their support) to explore the world and develop. *Most importantly parents do all of these things with their child; they are together, connected and alongside each other.* The principles that underpin the development of strong adult–child relationships in families also underpin Theraplay.

Structure, Engagement, Nurture, Challenge

There are four main themes that can be seen in everyday 'good enough' parenting which lead to healthy development. Theraplay builds upon these four themes. They are:

» *Structure*: about security and predictability, the adult being a reassuring and confident leader, helping to organise and support the child so that he can develop control over his body.

» *Engagement*: about the joy of companionship, being connected in the 'here and now', being focused on in a personal way.

» *Nurture*: about making the world feel safe and warm, reassuring the child that the adult will provide comfort, taking care of him so that he feels loved and valued.

» *Challenge*: about helping the child to develop, to feel confident and try new things, to pitch things at the right level for him and provide support to help him succeed.

As we suggest activities and approaches that may be helpful for your child, we will keep coming back to these four dimensions. A game may, for instance, be focused mainly on nurture and providing care, or it may be very structured and organised or perhaps designed to make your child laugh with you. The Theraplay approach is about understanding why these different ways of playing might help and about choosing what to focus on. These four dimensions will be described in more detail in Chapters 3–6. Before we move on to look at activities in more detail, we want to think about why Theraplay works and what theories it is based on. Let's look at this next.

Brain development and Theraplay

Our brains are extremely complicated but it can be helpful to think in some general ways about brain development when thinking about how to help your child. We will summarise some key ideas here for those of you who are interested. You can skip this part if it isn't helpful to you!

🖐 Your brain develops through your experiences, and especially through your important relationships.

Infants are born with an immature brain and need lots of different experiences in order to grow and develop. There are three important things to hold in mind:

1. Development happens in stages.

2. Parents are vital in helping their child develop.

3. The brain always checks for safety first.

Development happens in stages

Development happens in an ordered way, with layers of learning, so that new learning builds on what has happened before. Just as a baby learns to roll, then sit, then crawl before walking, so the building blocks of relationships develop in a similar way. Our baby gazes at us, emotionally connects, copies and joins in short 'to and fro' chats as the foundation for later communication. In the loving everyday care we provide for him, his brain is developing as he is learning. If he missed out on early stages of development, for whatever reason, then you may need to go back and fill in the gaps. You may need to 'go backwards to move forwards'. This can be the case even if you provided sensitive care. He may, for instance, need to revisit an earlier stage when he is facing a shift to a new stage and you will see younger needs expressed.

This idea, of layers of learning, is useful when you are trying to help your child learn new things, including learning about relationships. You have to start at the point where he is and move forward from there, to build on what has gone before. Theraplay uses this understanding in the way it 'builds success' into the play. Your child might be good at maths but find a simple 'to and fro' game hard. You observe carefully what he is comfortable with and find a way to play at that level, making the interaction successful. In that way, he can grow.

 There are steps in development that you can't just leave out. You might have to go back and 'fill in the gaps'.

The brain is organised 'from the bottom up and the inside out' with most basic functions developing first and then more complex ones developing later. The human brain is organised in three main levels of development. Here's a simplified model of the brain to give you an idea of what we mean.

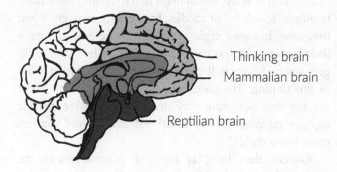

The bottom or most basic level is about everyday basic life functions and sensations: like breathing, heartbeat, digestion and body temperature; patterns like being awake and asleep and activity levels and how your senses pick up information. It is about survival. This level of the brain is working at birth. It is sometimes called the reptilian brain because even lizards and crocodiles have it.

Following from this survival or automatic function of the brain is the next level, which is sometimes called the mammalian brain because all mammals – like horses, cats and dogs – have it. This level is all about emotions and relationships and develops through relationships after the baby is born.

The final level is sometimes called the 'thinking brain' (which is mainly about humans) and this level is all about thinking about yourselves and others, developing verbal language and doing the sort of learning that is needed in school. This level develops as the child matures, and how it goes depends on how the earlier stages have gone. Babies and young children need safe adults to help them develop – they cannot do it on their own – and we will talk about this more in a moment.

As your child matures the higher levels of brain functioning develop, which helps him to control more basic impulses. Your baby or toddler, for instance, may cry when frustrated, but your eight-year-old may be able to cope a little better as he has more to draw on. When your child gets stressed, you will often see a return to earlier ways of functioning. The same happens to us! Just think about the last time you were very stressed or ill. Were you able to draw on your mature, 'adult' responses or did you feel more like a child?

Overall, the Theraplay approach concentrates on the first two developmental levels: the reptilian and mammalian parts. It is a nonverbal approach, which means that it's not about having conversations with your child. It is about helping you to help your child's body to become more regulated and organised, and helping you and your child with emotional relationship connection. Crucially, none of this can happen without your support.

 Theraplay starts at the bottom and works up. If your child is not able to regulate his body or rely on you as his parent then it is more important to focus on this part than on whether, for instance, he understands consequences for his behaviour. That will come later.

Parents are vital

We are all born with the most basic functions of the brain working and this allows us to survive. Taking into account individual differences in ability, how the baby develops from here depends to a great extent on his experiences, and most crucially his relationships with his parents. When you are caring for your baby, what happens, from a brain point of view, can be seen as you use your more mature brain to help calm your baby's brain. It is as if you 'lend your brain' to your child. Your baby is full of impulses and reactions, and you (as the more mature person who can appreciate what he might need) use the thinking and emotional part of your brain to help work out how to help him. As you provide sensitive care, the calmness and organisation of your response helps calm his more immature brain, so he settles. Your baby, for example, has a pain in his tummy and is screeching. You pick him up, and shush vigorously as you hold him firmly to your chest while making quick jiggling movements. Through your response, you are giving him the feeling that he is not alone in his pain and this helps his pain go down. As he begins to calm, you slow your movements and move to swaying, and you have a more soothing singsong voice, 'It's all right.'

This process, where you interpret what your child's needs are and then go on to provide them, happens all the time and in turn helps his brain to develop. Your baby and child cannot do this on his own. You will see throughout this book that we talk about your role in noticing what may be going on and working out how you can help your child.

Developing emotional connections and supporting your child to manage 'to and fro' interaction is fundamental to the Theraplay approach. Theraplay is about what happens between you, the interaction between two people. Both of you bring something to this. The Theraplay approach looks at what both of you bring to the interaction and tries to find ways to help you emotionally connect and get along well in a range of different ways. Once you feel you understand what is going on and have some ideas about how to support your child, then you can concentrate on the nonverbal 'here and now' experience of being together.

Safety comes first

We scan our environment for signs of danger at all times without realising it. By picking up information from all around us, we can decide whether we are safe (this all happens automatically so you will probably not be aware it is happening until something feels a bit wrong). If we are unsure (for instance, a stranger comes towards us), then we become more wary or vigilant and get ourselves prepared in case we need to do something to protect ourselves. In this state of mind, we will not feel relaxed or in the mood to play, explore or have fun because we have to make sure we're safe first.

If things get worse and we are in immediate danger then the survival response, 'fight, flight or freeze' gets switched on. This survival response occurs in all animals. Different animals might do different things in a danger situation, so a lion might fight, a horse run away and a rabbit stand still. We all use this part of the brain automatically and without thinking. For instance, if you were in an emergency situation, like a car crash, then lots of things change in your body and mind before you have a chance to think it through. This automatic survival part of your brain is switched on. If your child has had trauma in his early years, then you may see many signs that this part of his brain is on high alert. It's like the emergency switch is stuck on 'go'.

The Theraplay approach is very sensitive to what your child is expressing nonverbally through his body and is really focused on helping your child feel safe and comfortable. You try to pick up on early signs that he may be feeling anxious or frightened so you can then change what you are doing to help him feel safer. Our goal in Theraplay is to help your child spend more time in a relaxed and open state so that you can enjoy your relationship with each other.

We will now move on to talk a bit about the main theories that support Theraplay. You will see that there is a strong link to how the brain develops.

Main ideas that support Theraplay

There are many theories that are relevant and lots of recent developments in our understanding of the brain, which help us understand why Theraplay is so powerful. We will summarise some core ideas here.

We start by talking about babies because this is where relationships begin, but these ideas have relevance throughout life. Although it may look different at different ages, we all need emotional connection and people to rely on and share things with, throughout our lives.

The Theraplay approach focuses on:

> » forming an emotional connection with your child by concentrating on the earliest stage of relationship play, which is 'here and now' and to do with 'me and you together'.

> » understanding the attachment style of your child and gently challenging negative or stuck patterns through the play.

> » supporting your child to help him gain control over his body, impulses and feelings (regulation).

Forming an emotional connection

Most of us assume that we will automatically connect with and form a close relationship with our baby and child, but it doesn't always happen that way. Forming a genuine connection involves a lot of small things that need to go well. As a parent, you need to be able to read your child's signals and respond to him in a way that enables him to pick up and feel you responding. The timing, intensity, pace, style and way this all happens is like an intricate dance and involves both of you. Most of the time this connected 'relationship dance' happens completely naturally but even small mistimings can push things off track.

If you look at babies and parents interacting, or think of your own experience, you will see how amazingly detailed the relationship is – you look at your baby, he is looking away, you make a small noise to catch his attention, he turns his head, you say hello with a warm smile, he gurgles back. You are together, looking at each other with delight for a moment and you both feel the warmth and closeness of a genuine connection. It's a 'to and fro thing' between two people, like catching someone's eye when you share a joke, or squeezing a friend's hand when she is upset, or noticing a new freckle. How this connection looks will change as your child grows but the feeling is still the same. If the feeling could speak it would say, 'We're together, here and now, something is happening between us that feels good.'

This genuine connected experience may be very short or extend into a whole dance. In the normal give and take of relating, your baby will turn away when he needs a break so that he can regulate himself. When things go well in your relationship, you will know when he needs a break and when he is ready to reconnect again. Forming this emotional connection with your child is the bedrock of forming and maintaining the relationship.

It is not of course possible to be 'in-tune' or synchronised all of the time. Many everyday things, like the phone ringing or you having to stop your child from doing something, will break the feeling of connection. But usually you are able to sort out the situation quickly and you get things back on track with your child, you repair the break in connection. You might say, 'OK, you can tell me what it was you wanted now.' Most parents want to form a close relationship with their child but sometimes unexpected and unwanted events can get in the way and then this process of connecting can be much harder. If there is not enough of this genuine connection between you, or if you get disconnected too often and find it hard to get back together, then you may be facing difficulties in your relationship.

The Theraplay approach can help you to recreate this feeling of emotional connection in small and important ways. It can also help you notice your child in more detail and help you find ways to be with him so he can feel supported, valued and cared for. He can feel your deep interest in him.

 Being connected is a 'to and fro' thing. You feel warm, close and together.

Stages of relationship play

When we think about play we usually think about toys and imaginative play. It is, however, important to remember the earliest stages of relationship play. When you look at a parent and baby, a lot of what happens between them, from a connection point of view, is gazing, copying, touching and making noises. For the baby, the adult who loves him becomes his play focus. He wants to look at your face and play with your hair, to smile at you and have you smile back. Small games like blowing a raspberry on his tummy, Peek-a-boo or making up silly songs, are all focused on you getting to know each other and having fun together. This is the first stage of relationship development and comes before things like playing with toys and pretend play. Theraplay is about this first stage. Whatever the age of your child, there are ideas that can be adapted to recreate some of the feeling of this early kind of play.

If there are difficulties in your relationship, returning to this early stage in the way you play together can have a big impact because it is like putting back a missing piece or building up the foundations again. This is where you may see a difference between what happens in the Theraplay approach (where parent and child play simple interactive games together) and other play approaches which may be focused on toys, imagination and telling a story through play. The goal of Theraplay is to deepen your relationship with your child through building 'here and now' experiences of connection, using this early stage of development as its base.

 Returning to early and simple ways of playing together is like building up the foundations of your relationship.

Attachment theory

In the early months after a new baby arrives in the family, many parents say that it feels as if they are 'in a bubble' with their baby. Usually one parent does most of the caring for the baby during the first months, while the other parent and other family members have the essential role of providing support and keeping the family safe. For the parent and baby, it may feel it's 'just the two of us together'. You are building a profound relationship. How this early relationship goes has a big impact on how your baby starts to understand the world and how he feels about himself.

Let's take an example: Amy. Amy is a lucky baby. She has parents who are besotted and attentive, who are watching her carefully and trying to give her what she needs. What does Amy need? All the usual things we might provide for our young children: food, warmth, play, cuddles, routines, etc. It's a long list that most parents happily provide. Key within this list is safety. Amy's parents keep her safe. This is so important because without feeling safe, Amy won't be able to relax or explore and get to know the world. If Amy doesn't feel safe, then all of her energy will be spent on trying to survive.

How does Amy know that she is safe and cared for? Through many thousands of small interactions that happen every day. Something goes wrong (Amy has a tummy ache) and she begins to cry. Her parent responds and tries to work out what is wrong, maybe trying to cuddle or feed her or checking her nappy. While trying these things, Amy does a burp and she calms down in her parent's arms, she relaxes and all is well again. This mini-circle: baby upset, parent soothes, baby feels better, happens over and over again in the early months and develops into an expectation in the baby that this person is here to help me. Amy will look towards her parent for reassurance and will expect good things to come, comfort, play and security. This natural pattern has been described in different ways but the key is that the parent helps soothe the baby and becomes a safe base for the child.

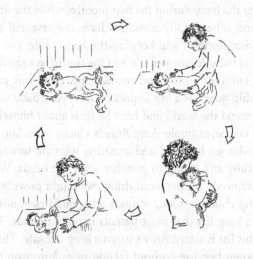

We see children using their parents as a safe base at all ages. When something goes wrong, for example, the door unexpectedly slams in the doctor's surgery, the toddler will automatically look to his parent for reassurance. Likewise, when a teenager receives a text from his parent wishing him good luck in an exam, it will help him calm. As adults, we all know how powerful it is to have someone alongside to comfort us when we are upset, rather than being upset alone.

The parent's response is the most important part in developing this safe base for the child. Over time, and through these thousands of small repeated cycles, children develop an idea about how they see themselves and others. For instance, if parents are sensitive and consistent in providing for their babies and children then children have the idea that they are safe, wanted, loved, and fun to be with ('I am nice and fun'), and they will look to others with an expectation of good things ('If I need help I can go to someone. People are kind'). This is the idea Amy will have about herself and the world, and it will lead her to try new things, seek help when she needs it, relax and grow. She will assume that her parents are there to support her. She will accept that they will be confident and kind leaders for her.

It doesn't matter whether a parent gets it right every time, it's the overall pattern of care that counts. What matters most is that the parent somehow resolves her child's discomfort most of the time. The child learns to feel secure with her parent.

Of course, things don't always go this well. For a wide range of reasons, a parent may not be able to provide this consistent and sensitive response to her baby and young child. What happens then?

Let's take an example: Joe. Joe is not such a lucky baby. The adults around him are stressed and the house is chaotic. He cries and no one comes, so he cries louder and longer. Eventually his parent comes but is irritated and rough in handling him so Joe becomes more and more upset until his parent shouts and then leaves him alone. Now Joe is alone and doesn't know what to do. He cries some more and when no one comes, eventually he gives up. He hasn't had the original distress soothed and now he is having to manage on his own and is miserable, confused and scared. Over time, if this pattern continues, Joe will learn that it is not worth calling out. He will try to manage things by himself and not expect to rely on his parents, even though he may be very small. And if we think about how he might come to feel about himself, Joe is likely to feel unimportant and uncared for ('I'm no good') and that others are not there to help him ('People don't help me, I've got to rely on myself').

These ways of seeing yourself, your parents and the world are sometimes described as attachment styles because once a pattern has become established it tends to stick. You can see how these styles affect everyday life as the child grows. As an example, a young child who is used to caring for himself will be reluctant to accept help from an adult; he might hurt himself and not cry or insist on doing everything on his own. When his parent is trying to help him to cross the road, he may refuse to hold her hand and say he can do it alone. Big fights can come about as he refuses to accept an adult's lead. A different example might be where a child has become passive and does anything anyone asks but without any emotion. He doesn't play or seem to be able to have fun.

 The way your close relationships went when you were young can have a big effect on how you see yourself and the world.

How can Theraplay help?

What we see is that a child brings his attachment style into the way he plays with someone. Instead of just being able to have fun and closeness with another person, your child might seem to be very domineering as if he is trying to 'spoil' or disrupt games, or alternatively he might be passive and compliant but 'switched off'. We need to 'look underneath' the behaviour to see that he might not know how to play any other way. A key principle in Theraplay is to build in success to make the play go well, without negativity or criticism. As the adult, you take responsibility for making it work out. The Theraplay approach gently challenges your child's insecure attachment style in the way you play together. For instance, you may find that games continually seem to go wrong with your child. His way of playing may be his way of coping with a lack of safety. It may be simpler for him to be in trouble than have the hope that things may turn out OK. When you find ways to make things go well within the play, this creates something new for him. Similarly, you might sensitively draw out your withdrawn child so that he can't resist but spontaneously join in with you.

As parents well know, it is easy to say 'go and play and have fun' but some children can't do this – things always seem to go wrong, someone is crying or left out. Sometimes, going back to simple play with a parent, when the parent works hard to make it successful, can have a big impact on helping your child to feel good about himself again; 'I can do this, I am fun to be with, I am a nice person.'

One of the things that makes it difficult for some children to play and form relationships easily is that they find it hard to control their body and emotions. They may 'blow hot and cold' and be impulsive, overactive and find it hard to calm down once they are excited. The ability to gain some control over the changes in your body and emotions is called regulation. When children have difficulties with regulation then Theraplay can also be very useful.

Developing control over your body and emotions – Regulation

We would all accept that babies need a lot of adult support but, as our child gets older, we expect him to be able to manage more, to be able to concentrate, be calm when needed and not to become out of control at the drop of a hat.

How does this internal control over your body develop?

Again, a major factor is the responsiveness of your parent in the early months. Human babies are born with an immature brain and they need the adults who care for them to help in connecting up the various parts. This happens through daily caring and practice. So, for instance, an infant may get very upset and will simply not know how to calm down. He needs his parent to pick up the signals and do practical things, like rocking him, singing, patting, feeding, drying him, etc. in order for his body to calm down. If he does have a responsive parent to help him, then after a lot of practice he will start to be able to calm more easily and to recognise what is going on inside his own body. His ability to regulate himself will develop. The more times his parent recognises that he is hot or cold, hungry, tired or in need of a cuddle, and provides that for him, the more he starts to feel this for himself. He picks up this understanding by having his needs sensitively met over and over again.

On the other hand, if he gets upset and there is no one to help him, he will get more and more distraught until he is exhausted. He won't have learnt anything except that he is scared and alone. When this happens often, then his body and emotions will be overwhelming for him, he doesn't know how to calm himself and things feel horrible. He doesn't know how to be in a calm state and will either go into overdrive (this is called hyper-arousal) or 'switch off' (this is called hypo-arousal).

It is easy to picture children who are hyper-aroused, jumping about, shouting, kicking, unable to focus or concentrate. It may be harder to notice children who are hypo-aroused, as they tend not to get involved in the action and are passive, distant and not showing interest. What we are aiming for is to help all children to be in the ideal state, where they can be calm and interested in what is going on around them, so they can take things in, have fun without going out of control, as well as relax and enjoy quiet times.

Hyper-aroused

Hypo-aroused

Children vary a great deal in how easy or difficult they are to soothe and how easily they can learn to regulate themselves. This is an area where many children struggle. Using Theraplay, you can practise going up and down in excitement and can help your overexcited child to calm or your unresponsive child come to life.

When you try to play with a child you quickly see the different states he may be in. He may, for instance, become overexcited by an activity (for example, when popping bubbles that have been blown into the air), and this can quickly turn into being out of control and aggressive. Parents in this situation often say they have stopped playing exciting games with their child because 'it always ends up in a fight'. This child clearly needs some help – he doesn't know how to calm down. It is a sad situation if fun games always go wrong.

What might we do with Theraplay? We would find ways to naturally calm your child by choosing activities that help him stay calm so he doesn't get too excited too quickly. When we play exciting games, we do it in a way which is organised to help him 'come down' once he has 'gone up'! Focusing on the state of your child in this way happens throughout any game you are playing and, as you become more experienced, you will find you can shift the energy levels and his overall state through your choice of games and the way you play with him.

For instance, instead of randomly blowing bubbles everywhere (your hyper-aroused child would find this much too exciting), we might say, 'See how many you can pop when you clap them.' If your child is still too excited and is jumping up and down, we add a bit more structure and focus in order to bring the excitement down. For example, we could sit him down and could capture just one bubble on the bubble wand and say, 'Show me your finger. Can you pop this bubble with that finger? Now a toe, can you pop this bubble with your toe?' In this way, your child automatically becomes calmer because he is having to focus. This happens without your child being told off or the game ending.

In everyday parenting, this can make a big difference. Once you, as a parent, become more able to pick up on what your child needs to help him gain a bit more control over his body and emotions, then life becomes much more predictable and enjoyable. The key is that adults have to help children do this first. If your child cannot do it (for whatever reason) he will not learn it on his own. He needs your help.

 Your child needs your help to know what is going on in his body.

The Theraplay approach concentrates on building awareness of these basic body functions by carefully observing your child's body responses and being sensitive in the way you play with him. Many of the Theraplay activities are focused on rhythm and pattern so that the activity has a pattern and a beginning, a middle and an end. It may also involve singing, touch and changes in energy from quiet to lively and back again. All of these sequences and patterns will be directly supporting his ability to regulate himself.

When life becomes difficult because of life events

There are times when family life can become more stressful for everyone and this can happen for a wide range of reasons, such as illness, bereavement, divorce, a house move or just a change in the stage of a child's development. When you are in the middle of a crisis it is very hard to do anything more than get through the situation. Once the dust has settled it can be very helpful to pay some attention to how your relationship is going with your child. Children often show their sadness and worry through difficult behaviour. You may find yourself becoming more easily irritated and distant just when he needs you the most. Returning to the ways you might have played with your child at an earlier age can be a very powerful way of rebuilding and repairing the strong connection between you. You may be surprised how some difficult behaviours will then fall away.

Summing up

This chapter has introduced how Theraplay was developed by being based on the things ordinary parents do when they lovingly raise their children. It draws upon some different theories and now has a lot of backup in terms of research and what we are learning about brain development. The approach is practical, easy to try out and doesn't need many materials.

Remember that the core feature of the Theraplay approach is about *connecting more deeply with your child.*

This deeper connection is achieved through engaging in playful activities with your child. Whether you use ideas from this book or invent your own is unimportant. Most families will have their own versions of the kinds of activities described. The key idea from Theraplay is that the activities are a vehicle to help you connect and get along well, so the specific activities, in themselves, don't matter. You may find that sharing a snack while watching a film or playing 'I spy' on a car journey works better than playing a specific activity outlined in this book, for example. The important part is that something you are doing together is helping you to feel closer to each other and remembering, especially when things are tough, that closeness and connection are crucial.

Parents who have taken on the Theraplay approach often say it has shifted their overall parenting style, 'like it's become a way of being in everyday life'. Many say they didn't think things could improve 'just through playing' and, although they may not understand why it works, it works. As one parent has said, 'It's hard to see why playing these simple and silly games would help, but it does.'

2

Getting Closer
to Your Child

The benefits of getting closer to your child may seem
obvious: you might get along better and have more fun,
your child might listen to you more easily and you might
share close, warm times together. Becoming closer as parent
and child may also raise understandable points such as:

> » I want her to manage in the outside world and she
>   will need to be independent so I don't want to
>   protect her too much. She needs to stand on her
>   own feet in the end.

> » If we are too close then how will I discipline her?
>   Doesn't she need to be a bit scared in order to take
>   notice of me and to respect me?

> » She likes playing young games but it doesn't seem
>   appropriate for her age. She should be doing more
>   grown up things by now. I don't want to 'baby' her.

We all hope that our children will love us and that we will
be the best parents we can for them. At the same time,
because children change so much as they grow up, we will
have different expectations of what they might do and
what our relationship with them might be like at different
ages. When they are small, we hope we can cuddle and
comfort them, that we can provide for them and help

them get into routines so they can settle. As they become toddlers and start to say 'no', we realise that they need help in learning how to follow an adult lead, and how to manage frustration. As they get to school age, we hope that they will start to become more independent, learn new skills (perhaps from us!) and take important steps forward. We hope that they are able to have friends and that they are more able to share and understand another person's point of view. As they approach adolescence, we hope that they will start to understand more about the world, about relationships and themselves, and that they will mature into confident and caring adults.

So, parenting changes a lot as your child grows. Some of us might feel more confident with babies and feel out of our depth with teenagers, or the other way around. It can be hard to keep connected and close to your child across all these different stages, especially as they get older and seem to want to pull away from you.

Why does having someone to be close to, and rely on, matter?

Throughout our lives, we need people to feel close to, who we can enjoy spending time with and who we can rely on when things go wrong. When our relationships go well, it is a wonderful thing. As anyone who has faced extreme situations will say, at the end of the day, it's the people closest to you that count.

How do we learn how to be close to others? After all, it comes with risks. You may be let down or hurt. We learn about closeness and intimacy in our early years. When we are infants, we are totally reliant on those caring for us to keep us safe and meet our needs. As we grow and begin to explore the world, there is a natural pull away from our main carer. This pulling away from those we are close to, and then coming back when we need to reconnect, happens throughout life.

Jack, aged two, ventures further away from you as he becomes more confident, but when something goes wrong (for example, he climbs a bit too high), he calls for help and you are quickly by his side to help. This small example is repeated many thousands of times across the years as Jack grows up and he becomes sure that he has someone in his life who will be there to support him if he needs them. It is this long tried and tested period of relying on another person that allows him to branch out and try new things. Relying on someone else and being able to explore go together. If one is going well, then the other can grow. Without feeling secure and protected, it is hard to learn new things. All of your energy is taken up in checking you are safe. So, helping your child to rely on you actually leads to greater independence later on.

 If you have someone you can turn to, you can feel safe enough to try new things.

Becoming close to your child happens in lots of different ways, through caring for her (washing, feeding, cuddling, rocking, helping), having fun together (laughing, playing), sharing experiences (happy or sad) and through finding ways to make up and repair when things go wrong.

You can just feel it

The thing about being close to someone is that it is something you feel inside. It can be hard to explain and might not seem logical. It is not always to do with spending a lot of time together, more about whether the person 'gets' you and you feel their warmth in some way.

> » Think about people you feel close to, what is it about being with them that gives you that close feeling?

> » When you have had a difficult time with someone, what is it that helped you to get that close feeling back?

We might have very different answers to these questions, such as:

'It's my dad who I felt closest to. Even though he wasn't around much he really "got me". I felt he really liked me.'

'I love my friend. She just knows how to cheer me up and make me feel special.'

'My mum somehow knows when I'm not OK, I don't know how she does that. If things go wrong I always know I can go back home.'

When you think about getting closer to your child, some key themes often come up again and again. These are:

> » providing care and touch.

» sharing things together – having fun and sharing experiences.

» helping your child when they are upset or stressed.

» repairing when things go wrong.

The Theraplay approach includes all of these different ways for you and your child to feel closer to each other. Theraplay focuses on finding direct and nonverbal ways of getting closer. These nonverbal experiences are the ones which give you a gut feeling of closeness, something that feels genuine, real and in the 'here and now'. Building up this feeling of closeness with your child brings a lot of joy and also gives you something to fall back on when times are hard. We will look at these ideas in turn.

Providing care and touch: Touch within Theraplay

Touch is a fundamental part of feeling close and many Theraplay activities involve some kind of touch. Touch is a normal, healthy part of what happens between a child and parent. It is hard to imagine how anyone could care for a baby and toddler without there being some sort of touch. You touch your baby to wash, feed and dress her and to change her nappy. You also rock and cuddle her, support her head and move and hold her in ways that are safe and kind.

These different kinds of touch are essential to your baby's development. Research which has looked at what happens to baby animals when they are not touched by their parent shows that the absence of touch, or harmful touch, leads to a whole host of problems including poor physical growth. Healthy touch is an essential ingredient for a baby to grow well.

Of course, the way you touch your child changes as she develops and you will naturally adapt. In addition to the touch involved in basic care such as dressing, hugs and cuddles, as your toddler starts to explore she needs touch to keep her physically safe. She has learned to walk and can suddenly explore the world in ways that may put her in danger. Curious toddlers usually want to climb, run and get into things! Her need to explore knows no limits; she is too young to be aware of the possible dangers so it's your job to keep her safe. You might pick her up and take her away from the danger or hold her on your lap. You will need to hold her hand for safety. This kind of touch is practical and clear and helps her to feel that someone bigger and wiser than her is making things safe, so that she can relax and be young.

As your child grows, touch continues to be an important and natural part of her relationship with you. She is learning to ride a bike and needs your physical support to stabilise her while she tries something new.

Touch can also be very nurturing and provides emotional support. How much better does it feel to cry on someone's shoulder than to cry alone? It has been suggested that touch is our first language and that even before we can see, smell, taste or hear, we experience others and ourselves through touch. Touch is essential for forming an emotional bond with another. It also helps us to cope with difficulties because safe and kind touch can be stress relieving and calming. Touch, such as a hug from a safe person, can even reduce feelings of depression and anxiety.

 Healthy touch is essential for healthy development.

Within the Theraplay approach, healthy touch is used as a natural part of many activities. For most children, they will enjoy this and the feeling of closeness and connection it brings. For others, it may be hard.

When touch becomes difficult

Your child may find touch hard for a wide variety of reasons. Maybe she experienced a difficult birth and medical interventions, which have linked touch to pain rather than to comfort. Maybe she has been born with a high level of touch sensitivity, or perhaps when she was small her parents weren't able to be sensitive in the way they handled her. She may have experienced inadequate or even abusive forms of touch in her early years, which have led to confusing beliefs about what touch means. For whatever reason, some children (and adults) find aspects of touch or physical contact with another person difficult.

How can you help?

Think about how your child reacts to different types of touch. Some children seem to crave a lot of physical contact and touch while others can shy away or avoid it. She might be very sensitive to light touch but fine with something firmer. You might try to go towards her and she moves away from you, or when she comes towards you she bashes into you too hard and then it doesn't feel good. It can be difficult to know how to respond to different sensitivities about touch. The first step is to really get to know your child by watching her and really thinking about how she responds.

Simple checklist: How does your child respond to touch?

See if these sound like your child:

- ✓ She can't tell if her face is dirty.
- ✓ She hugs too hard and often breaks things, like pencils, by pressing too hard.
- ✓ She chews or mouths everything, like cuffs and collars on her clothes.
- ✓ She constantly touches people and things.
- ✓ She drops objects frequently.
- ✓ She likes to be barefoot.

If you ticked these then your child may be under-responsive to touch. This means that she can't feel things very well and may have to touch more, press hard or push herself against things, to feel that they are there.

Now consider whether these sound like your child:

- ✓ She hates being tickled or cuddled.
- ✓ She gets annoyed if somebody 'accidentally' touches her.
- ✓ She doesn't like having her hair washed and brushed.
- ✓ She avoids messy play and doesn't like having things like paint and sand on her hands.
- ✓ She is fussy about the texture of her clothes.

If you ticked these, then your child may be over-responsive to light touch. This means that she is very sensitive to touch and it may be painful for her and she reacts to small things as they make her anxious. It may mean that lots of things, like people brushing up against her or being in noisy and busy places, will be hard.

Sometimes the way your child responds to touch can be complicated and it might be worth getting a proper assessment to see if your child has sensory processing difficulties (for example with an occupational therapist). Children who have experienced trauma (including medical procedures), poor early care and children who have difficulties such as autism often have problems around touch and movement. It is important to understand your child's difficulties properly so that you can help her. You might think she is being difficult or seems to be rejecting you when actually she is struggling with what is going on in her body. For example, you go to hug her and she moves away. You might feel upset and rejected when actually her reaction is because she doesn't like the feeling of being touched. It's not to do with her not liking you.

In Theraplay, touch is used in different ways across the different dimensions and you might find that some ways of using touch work better than others with your child. The important thing is to notice how she responds, adjust what you do to make it as manageable as possible for her and keep trying.

Try keeping touch practical and a natural part of an activity. Don't make a fuss over it. Keep calm, clear and confident and avoid tickling and teasing. The core message from Theraplay is that touch always needs to be kind and safe. Touch and physical contact should always be for the benefit of your child.

Sharing things together: Having fun and sharing experiences
Quick quiz

» Do you have fun with your child?

» Does it feel genuine and two way?

» Can you relax with your child and enjoy each other's company in ordinary day-to-day ways?

» Can you share sad as well as happy experiences?

The most memorable moments in life are usually those where we felt genuinely affected by something, whether good or bad. When this happens in a positive way with someone we love, then it deepens our relationship. Think about a time when you were with someone you cared about and you both couldn't stop laughing or you had a tender experience together. The connection between you in that moment feels physical. Something happens in both of your bodies that is like a mirror of each other. You are together sharing the experience.

 When you share a 'here and now' experience, the connection between you feels physical. It's just me and you together.

This is similar to the kinds of play you might share with your baby or toddler. You bounce her on your knee (getting into a rhythm and spirit of the game) and then do something exciting and she bursts into laughter. This is a moment of joint spontaneous delight. Both of you are filled with warmth and joy, her belly giggles are catching and you laugh too. She looks at you with clear love and openness and you look back and, in that moment, it's just you and her sharing this small and important experience together. These kinds of experiences may be brief (you can't be in this state all of the time) but they are vital. They are vital so that you form this close bond together, vital to help her experience joy and well-being, and vital to help her experience changes in her body state in a way which is manageable.

Change and surprise

For many of us, changes and surprises can be enjoyable: going on holiday, taking a lunch break, having a surprise visit. All of these things can be refreshing and exciting. Many of the greatest moments of delight happen at moments of surprise. When you pretend to playfully 'drop' your toddler or go to shake someone's hand and move it away at the last moment or crack a joke, it is the element of surprise that often creates the amusement.

Many of the best-loved children's games and songs will have a sudden change of rhythm in them to give this surprise and delight feeling and many of the Theraplay games include some element of anticipation and surprise. The moment of surprise can bring about a body feeling of your tummy flipping, an 'ooooh' and a giggle.

For some children, however, change and surprise can bring anxiety or fear and she will prefer to keep things the same, to know what is happening next and to avoid situations where she is not in control of what is going on. You may see her trying to take charge of situations, being reluctant to try anything new, keeping to plans and rituals, becoming angry if things change. Behaving in this way will work in some ways because she will know what is going to happen next but it also reduces the variety of her experiences, makes changes in routine hard and means less spontaneity. It is important to remember that underneath this kind of rigid behaviour is anxiety, and so to move forward you need to find a way to help her feel less anxious.

One key idea from Theraplay is that of *safe surprises* – finding ways to introduce a tiny surprise within a familiar game that will be enjoyable rather than unpleasant for your child. If you think about it, the body feeling of excitement is not so different from the body feeling of anxiety or fear. If you are someone who worries about what is coming up next, then the anticipation of the surprise (which is supposed to be exciting) will not feel good either. Within Theraplay, this idea of providing a safe surprise is built carefully into the activities. For instance, a simple and organised game of dropping a bean bag from your head into your child's hands may be popular for a child who likes to know what's happening. The game is clear and she can see the bean bag, she understands what is going to happen and nothing is going to suddenly come up behind her and alarm her. You say, 'I'll drop the bean bag when I say blue. Green, brown (slight pause), blue!' You then drop the bean bag. The wait for the 'blue' signal will be short enough to keep her interest and long enough to give her some feeling of anticipation. It might not look very exciting to you, but to her it's just right. Within this understanding of the game, she may start to be able to enjoy this small element of surprise.

Obviously, for a more confident and lively child you may need to be quicker and bigger in your level of excitement to keep her with you. The principle is the same: you're trying to provide a moment of genuine connected delight that you are sharing together, a 'now moment' between you which feels good.

Sharing tender and quiet times

There are many ways of being together and connected which are calmer and quieter, and these are just as important. This happens in everyday life when you are doing ordinary things alongside each other like cooking, eating, walking and watching TV. In Theraplay there will be times of activity and times of quiet. The calmer activities try to create a feeling of being absorbed and together in the activity. There are a range of activities which can be very still and quiet and bring a feeling of calmness and peace to what you are doing together (like the activity 'Sticker match', where you put a sticker on your child and she puts one on you so that it is like a mirror image). Activities that specifically focus on nurture also aim to create intimacy and closeness in a quiet way, and any singing or speaking-out rhymes can have a similarly meditative impact. In these quiet and concentrated kinds of activities you can relax and just be together.

Helping your child when they are upset or stressed

Have a look at these questions in our quick quiz.

Quick quiz

» Do you know when your child is upset or stressed? How do you tell?

» Can your child come to you or show you when she is upset or stressed? Does she?

» Are you able to comfort her in some way?

» Do you think she feels you will help her without judging her or feeling disappointed?

You can see that the answers to these questions will vary according to your child's age. Your four-year-old might graze her knee and come to you crying whereas your 15-year-old who has had a bad day might not tell you what is up but you may notice and make her a cup of tea. The important part is that you can pick up when she is not OK and that you can find a way to help her in some way.

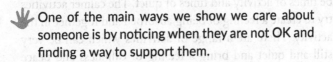 One of the main ways we show we care about someone is by noticing when they are not OK and finding a way to support them.

Within the Theraplay approach there are many chances for you to show your child that you have noticed that she is struggling, and you can then provide her with some support to help her through that moment. This is particularly the case when activities involve some level of challenge. We (and our children) often set our expectations too high, and without thinking we put pressure on her to succeed.

Try to pitch expectations so that you build in success and, if she is finding it hard and needs an extra bit of support or encouragement, then try to give this when you see the early signs of stress. Through the play, she will get the feeling that you do notice and can help.

In almost any activity, your child may show signs that she is feeling stressed. It might be that she is finding it hard, is worried about getting it wrong, or that her body is becoming agitated or overexcited, perhaps she pulls away or slightly flinches. Whatever it is, this is your opportunity to notice, to show her that you notice and to provide some support. The idea is that this will transfer into other more important situations.

Repairing when things go wrong

When your relationship with your child is going well what usually happens is that you muddle along in daily ways together. You may have times when there is playfulness and fun and also times when things go wrong. In all parent–child relationships, things are bound to 'go wrong' sometimes, at least from the perspective of your child! Any time you tell her off, ask her to do something she doesn't want to do or stop her from doing something she does want to do, there will be a break in the closeness. She will be angry or upset and whether she shows you this or not, you will feel the change in your relationship. What you usually do is wait a short time before the two of you get back on track together. The 'repair' in the connection between you after these breaks is very important.

When your relationship is strong, the repair usually happens without too much difficulty. For example, you might acknowledge that you got too cross, she might apologise or show that she feels sorry. When your relationship is more fragile, or your child is more vulnerable, it can be much harder to repair things after even a minor break. Something quite small can quickly turn into a major incident. For instance, you have to cancel an outing to the park because it has got too late. Although you may have an excellent explanation (and she may have caused the lateness), to her it is a betrayal and broken promise and she withdraws in a state of high distress saying that she no longer trusts you. Even if you try to reconnect, it can feel as though she wants nothing more than to withdraw for ever. For some parents, these high dramas around any break in the connection with their child can seem to make up a big part of their daily lives.

Theraplay gives many opportunities for repairing breaks in connection in a much less intense way than these kinds of incidents, and can help your child experience that coming back together is possible when things have gone wrong. Theraplay has a 'no hurts' rule. When something goes wrong in a game, you would stop the game, acknowledge someone is hurt and re-do it in some way which feels like a repair of the situation. This applies to physical 'hurts' as well as emotional ones. So, for instance, if during a game of 'Beep and honk', your child presses hard on your nose and it hurts you, you might say, 'Ow, that was a bit hard, let's try again.' Then, when you do it again, you would hold her finger and support her to press your nose so that it is done without hurting you, 'Beep, that's it.' We try not to tell children off and risk shaming them but to redirect and find ways to complete the sequence in a constructive way.

Another opportunity to repair occurs when you think you have done something that she doesn't like. For instance, you snuggle up too close and she looks uncomfortable. You might say, 'I'm sorry, that was too much, I'll move over here.' Remember that the important part is that you are looking out for clues that she is not OK and, if she can't say it out loud or show you clearly, then you need to watch her body behaviour. You have to really concentrate on her nonverbal responses. She may smile at you but be holding her body tense, so she is not OK even though she is smiling. You want to notice her tense body and show her that you have seen that she is not comfortable. A different child may of course show you directly by shouting or hitting out.

If you have caused this discomfort, then this is the time to repair by recognising that it was you who made her feel uncomfortable. You might say, 'I'm sorry, I made that too hard and it's made you feel bad, let's do it a different way.' Getting the hang of repairing and taking responsibility when you have made mistakes can go a long way to supporting your child. It will start to feel OK for mistakes to happen once you both know you can get back on track afterwards. You will need to show your child that you can do this first before expecting her to be able to do it.

 If you can make up and repair when things go wrong then your relationship will feel much stronger.

Summing up

Most parents want to feel close to their children but this can be difficult for a wide range of reasons. If you take the long view of what you want to achieve as a parent, most of us would wish that our children will love us, will feel loved and will want a relationship with us as they grow up. Unfortunately, the everyday efforts of family life can often get in the way of closeness and sometimes the very things that might make us feel close are the things that end up in a fight. For example, a parent may say:

When it comes to brushing her hair or teeth or mealtimes, we always have a massive clash, I can't help it, I just end up trying to force her and then we are both angry and it's horrible and the opposite to what it's supposed to be.

In your dreams, you might have imagined that you would sit and brush her hair, help her with her teeth or share an enjoyable meal. The reality may be quite different. Family life is rarely straightforward.

The message here is 'don't give up' the effort of trying to connect and recapture some closeness even if it is very brief. This might be through laughter, cuddling up, helping her through a difficult time or making up after an argument. When you are able to create small moments of this connection and closeness together it can feel like gold dust, and where there is a little gold dust, more may come.

3

Structure

In this chapter, we look at how structure is defined in Theraplay and why it's important for our children and us as parents. Then we look at why it sometimes goes astray and what we can do to re-establish it with our child using ideas from Theraplay.

What is structure?

The element of structure is a core part of Theraplay and is based upon what ordinary parents naturally do. In Theraplay, structure is focused on how we do four things:

» We set up basic sequences and routines for attending to our child's basic needs.

» We help our child's body to become regulated and organised.

» We play with our child, using activities that have sequences and rhythms.

» We look after our child's basic safety by setting limits and providing guidance.

Let's take a closer look at what this all means.

Setting up basic sequences to meet basic needs

In previous chapters, we looked at how you spend the early days and weeks being focused on getting to know your baby and learning about what he needs. You start to develop basic sequences and routines for feeding, changing nappies and settling him for sleep. The various tasks, such as the many nappy changes, become very familiar sequences which have clear beginnings and ends. Each day tends to become full of predictable sequences and patterns, which helps your baby learn about when to be awake, when to sleep, when to eat and when to relax and look around to explore his new surroundings. Your baby cannot do any of these things on his own. He needs you. You make life become familiar and predictable.

Regulating and organising your child's body

As a sensitive and responsive parent, your care and attention to your baby in the early days and months helps your baby's body to become physically more regulated and predictable. In other words, he's not 'all over the place'. He is no longer such a bundle of impulses but is beginning to build up sequences of organised interaction. For instance, over all of the many times when you respond to your baby's cries, by recognising the cry and feeding him in a predictable way, he becomes able to understand what hunger and fullness mean. These everyday caring responses may seem simple but they are actually critical for your baby to be able to become organised and regulated in his own body.

Play activities have sequences and rhythms

As you spend time with your baby, you also begin to play in ways that have a bit of a sequence. For example, when your baby does something funny, like sticking his tongue out, you copy him and he copies back and, before you know it, you are taking turns playfully in a predictable way. When he begins to coo and babble, you may babble and 'talk' back, and before you know it you're sharing a conversation together.

These early play sequences are the beginnings of your child learning to play with another person in a 'to and fro' kind of way. As your child grows, you play with him in ways that involve rhythm and a clear pattern. Many common nursery action songs provide this. The popular 'round and round the garden' rhyme has a clear beginning, middle and end. Young children find this very engaging and are usually happy to hear it from you again and again. Predictable feels good. If you were to take a stroll along the library bookshelves for preschoolers you would see that many simple picture books involve rhythm, simplicity and predictable endings. These provide much needed experiences of structure for your young child.

Looking after your child's safety by setting limits and being his guide

If you think about what we, as parents, do much of the time when raising our child, a lot is about supporting him to do the everyday things that need to happen, like getting dressed, coming to the meal table, brushing teeth, holding hands when crossing the road. All of these things require a level of organisation and predictability. They become routines which go well when you and your child both go along with the idea that you are leading the way.

As the grown-up, you are the one who has learned how to look after yourself and live safely within the world. Your child has not yet learned this and so needs guidance from you, especially when he is faced with new things. For him, everything is unknown and brand new, so he needs you to show him the way and keep him safe.

You are also the one who helps your child to learn how to manage his feelings and behaviour, which at times can feel really big for him. We have probably all heard the phrase 'terrible twos', which is associated with the stage when our toddler throws huge tantrums over seemingly trivial things, such as something he wants to do and we have said 'no'. This is a stage of child development when your child begins to feel the power of his emotions and he realises that he has some control over his body. He can walk, run and shout! You, however, realise that the intensity of the tantrum is way too big for the circumstances so you begin to help him to manage these feelings, by perhaps distracting him away from that wanted toy. You know that you need to set some limits for him as he is not yet wise enough to make safe choices. You would not let him choose all of the shopping in your weekly basket. You would also not let him decide when it's safe to cross the busy road. By being a parent who sets limits and boundaries, you are keeping him safe and helping him to learn about what is OK.

Structure throughout childhood

As your child grows, most parents find that their provision of structure also changes. When your toddler starts to move and explore the world, you begin to put in limits so that he is safe. For example, you will physically stop him from putting his fingers in the plughole or eating the woodlouse, and so on. As he grows into an older child, he may not need you to hold his hand any more while crossing the road but he still needs you to be a clear guide for him. He still needs you to help him regulate and provide a structure for the day. For instance, with your older child, you decide when it's time for him to get off the video game and go to bed.

At each stage of development, right through to adulthood, we need to find ways to provide sufficient structure for our child so that he feels safe and life feels predictable. As we provide this consistent structure, so he develops more control over his body and emotions; we call this becoming regulated.

Families are all different. The way each family uses structure and what feels right will be unique to each parent–child pair and each family, and it will differ too across cultures. When things go well, there is a creation of routines, organisation and expectations in the family environment. This helps everyone to feel safe and secure. Within the main family relationships, you, as the adult, create a feeling of stability for your child, by being a safe and confident leader, knowing him, timing things right, changing activity and calming things down when needed. This helps your child to develop his own internal control over himself.

Why structure is helpful to children: The child's perspective

Children of all ages thrive when they are living within environments that are safe and predictable. As children learn about themselves and the world, they will watch the adults around them, follow and take guidance from them.

Having a strong, kind parent as leader and guide helps your child feel safe and regulated within his body and in the world. Your child receives the message, 'You are a child and are young. I am here looking after you. I know what you need and this is what we're going to do.' It feels good for him to know that you have everything in hand for him.

If you were to watch any group of young children who have a confident and trusted adult leading them, the children will look relaxed and calm. They know how nice it feels to be led and organised by someone who knows them. As children grow older the form this takes may change but, at any age, being with someone who takes a positive lead and makes things happen is very reassuring.

Why structure is helpful to parents: The parent's perspective

We all tend to do better when our lives are predictable and we feel in control and competent. As a parent, it feels good to be the one who is structuring and leading your child. You really know your child as an individual, know how to support him and can lead with sensitivity. When this goes well it enhances your confidence, creates clear expectations and you feel as though you are 'doing your job' well. Family life will always have elements of surprise and unpredictability in it, but overall the pattern and organisation of your family will help stabilise things afterwards.

It is important not to confuse this kind of adult leadership with more negative approaches, where it can feel as though the adult is just trying to control and dominate the child. This is not how Theraplay sees structure. The Theraplay idea is that through a positive, clear, confident and playful approach, we become strong, kind and sensitive 'leaders' for our child. This gives us, as parents, a clear role which can feel intrinsically good, and helps our child to feel safe and well organised.

 We all need structure and predictability in order to feel safe.

When structure goes wrong or astray

For some children and parents, establishing a comfortable level of structure is difficult. This can be because of vulnerabilities in the child, the adult or often a combination of both. We look at some reasons below.

Why a child may find structure difficult

There are many reasons why a child may find structure difficult:

» Children are all different. Your child may prefer a more flexible approach and find it hard when you need to be organised or things have to be structured.

» Your child may have difficulties which make it hard for him to control his body and his impulses.

» Your child may have experienced early trauma, such as parenting which has been chaotic or neglectful. He might have little or no experience of a predictable life. Being chaotic will then feel more familiar to him.

» Your child may be on the autism spectrum and prefer very high structure.

It can be helpful to think about how your child responds to structure. This child checklist will help you think about this.

Child checklist: How does your child respond to structure?

✓ Does your child accept it when you take the lead?

✓ Does your child seem to struggle to know what you want him to do?

✓ Does your child follow your lead (without fear or anxiety)?

✓ Does your child insist on doing things his own way?

✓ Does your child seem to end up being the one in charge?

✓ Do activities seem to end in chaos?

Some children, for whatever reason, need more help and experience with structure. It could be useful to think about how you can start adding some Theraplay activities into family life.

Why parents may find structure difficult

Parents can sometimes struggle with structure for different reasons:

» You may be someone who tends to be disorganised or doesn't feel comfortable setting limits.

» You may currently feel unwell or be experiencing difficulties, which make daily life disorganised and unpredictable.

» Your own experience of how your parents treated you when you were growing up can have a big influence. Maybe you had parents who were overly strict and disciplined and you don't want to be like them, or perhaps they were very relaxed and you don't really know how to add more structure. This can sometimes make it hard to work out how to provide structure for your child in a clear, confident and sensitive way.

» There are also many life events (like divorce or illness within the family), which lead to changes in how your family usually runs and organises itself.

Families are also very different. Some families seem to manage with low levels of structure and all goes well. The opposite is also true so it is important not to be too simplistic about what is the 'right' level of structure. Children are all different too. Some children need more structure than other children.

Many parents have told us that when family life is too chaotic, both parents and children are more likely to be unhappy, to 'lose it' and to become out of control. If you are feeling as though your family life has become chaotic, then we have some ideas about how you can begin to take more leadership and create a more loving and playful atmosphere within your home.

If levels of parenting structure are too low or too high for your individual child, then you could see some problems. For example, if you do not provide enough structure for your child, or your child can't follow your lead, then family life can fall apart very quickly. With very low structure you may see your child become overactive, chaotic, getting overstimulated easily and wanting to be in control. Sometimes, as parents, we may be disorganised ourselves, have difficulty with setting limits or with being a confident leader. Sometimes, we can rely too much on talking and expecting our child to listen to us. Sometimes we might not read our child's signals well and we might be too exciting or not exciting enough.

In contrast, when you have very high structure, your child may become withdrawn or lacking in spontaneity. There is also a risk that you can become too critical or harsh. Although you may feel that being very strict is a way of being in charge and leading, if your child is withdrawn or unhappy then you may need to lower your levels of structure so that your child can relax and play.

It can be helpful to think about the level and type of structure that you provide to your child. This parent checklist provides some helpful questions to consider.

Parent checklist: What's your structure like?

- ✓ Do you think you provide a clear lead?

- ✓ Do you feel mainly in control of your family life?

- ✓ Do you rely a lot on rewards and threats to influence your child?

- ✓ Has family life become full of verbal commands or detailed negotiations?

- ✓ Do you sometimes find it difficult to set limits with your child?

- ✓ Do you sometimes feel that you could 'lose it' with your child?

The parent checklist may have highlighted some issues for you in relation to structure. Most parents will, from time to time, find it difficult to establish the right level of structure in family life. Being a parent is demanding and our child's needs change. This can make it tricky to keep up the right level of structure.

What does structure look like when it's present?

Here are some signs that you and your child have developed more structure together:

- » You are providing clear guidance which fits with what your child needs and is able to do.

- » Your child accepts and seems more relaxed when you take the lead.

Remember though that structure is not about being dominant or overly strict with your child. It is about being a calm and clear guide. One way to ensure that you are not becoming too strict or controlling is to also increase nurture with your child alongside any increase in structure. We look at nurture in a later chapter. In fact, as you will realise more while reading this book, all of the four dimensions work together hand-in-hand.

What can you do? Structure ideas from Theraplay

There are a lot of small but important things that you can do to increase structure and to give your child the feeling that you are leading and that you know what you are doing. Everything in Theraplay is done in a playful way, which means that increasing structure is not about being strict or having battles with your child. Instead it is about finding playful ways to:

» have positive times with your child with you being the leader.

» create a feeling of predictability and pattern with activities that have a beginning, middle and end such as, 'We'll sort the washing, then feed the animals, then go out to play'.

» use nonverbal ways of making things happen, like putting your hand on his arm as you move forward.

» ensure that your child knows what is happening and what you are expecting from him – make expectations specific such as, 'Put the cup on the side, thanks.'

Here are some things for you to try:

» Reduce your use of language and questions. Instead of 'Could you?' say, 'Let's do this.'

» Show your child what's needed rather than tell him. For example, pick him up or provide a supportive hand to him rather than enter into negotiations.

» Build in enough practical support to ensure success. For instance, 'Time to put your shoes on (you help to make it happen), that's it.'

» Stay in the 'here and now' with a positive and confident attitude and avoid bribes and penalties.

» Try using signals (saying, 'ready steady go' or 'when I say yellow') to start and end things, and change the pace during an activity.

The sorts of specific activities that are helpful in practising a feeling of structure are those with a pattern, where the adult is the one who is in the lead.

One example of an activity that involves leadership, predictability and rhythm is the game of Hand-stack. Let's look at what this involves and why we think it's a great example of structure.

Hand-stack

Hand-stack involves a parent and child taking it in turn to place one hand on top of the other's hand so that their hands make a tower which climbs higher and higher. There are different ways that you can take the lead in this game. You might say whose turn it is to place their hand next and organise or change the speed of the game, such as saying, 'Ooh let's be really slow!' When you play in this way, your child experiences you as being the one leading the game while having fun. This can feel very different to other parts of his day when he is told to do things like, 'Put your coat on!' A Theraplay way of asking him to put his coat on might be something like, 'Let's see if you can zip up your coat and put on your hat before I get to Q in the alphabet song.' He follows your lead but it feels warm and connected. Since children learn more through experience than words, simple games like the Hand-stack can provide a regulating and predictable experience that feels fun and provides a practice model for other times when he will follow an adult lead.

In Theraplay, we think about how we can use structured games to give our child the experience of our being his guide and lead. Let's look at an example of how Theraplay could help an over-controlling child.

Example: John

John wanted to be in control of everything. Whatever his dad wanted him to do, he argued against. They were at almost constant loggerheads with battles over getting up, having breakfast, leaving the house, and so on. You can imagine they were not having much fun. As every day became a series of conflicts, John's dad became more and more frustrated. John looked as if he was enjoying this situation, laughing at his dad. Dad was feeling useless and at a loss as to what to do. Punishments had no effect and rewards only worked for as long as John wanted something. What could he do? John didn't look like he was unhappy (he was laughing), but actually underneath he was feeling very anxious. Things felt all wrong. John did not know how good it felt to have an adult be in charge and Dad didn't know how to change things. Both of them were feeling out of control.

Dad tried a Theraplay approach. Instead of getting into an argument, he tried to be playful and take the lead. Dad said that he would race him to the bathroom, he made his breakfast into a funny design, he decided how the morning atmosphere would go (working hard to keep himself calm) and made it happen. John was very surprised. Why would Dad be like this when he was trying to have a fight? He was confused and then he joined in. He couldn't quite resist. If there was to be a race against the clock putting shoes on, then he would definitely be able to do it within 30 seconds. Something was changing. Dad was leading, taking charge of the atmosphere and John could begin to relax a bit. He was only small after all.

Ideas from Theraplay to increase structure

Table 3.1 gives some ordinary life examples of structure and some activities from Theraplay for you to try. Full descriptions of all of the Theraplay activities here are given in Chapter 10.

Table 3.1: Structure: Ordinary life and Theraplay activities

Age	Ordinary life example of adult-led structure	Theraplay activities to promote structure
Infant	Rocking, establishing wake–feed–sleep patterns, holding baby so he is comfortable	Mirroring; Patty-cake; songs with beginning, middle and end
Toddler	Holding hands to cross road, saying no, setting routines, providing age-appropriate environment	Bean bag drop; Blanket run; Jump into my arms; Play dough squeeze
Primary age	Sitting for meals, getting ready for school, joining with a group	Hand-stack; Pop the bubble; Copy funny faces; Follow the leader; Draw around hands and feet; Three-legged walk
Teen	Providing a predictable routine and meals, setting house rules, getting him out of bed	Cotton ball blow; Measuring; Eye signals

Summing up

In this chapter, we have looked at what structure is from a Theraplay perspective, why it is important for our child and for us as parents. We have thought about why structure is sometimes hard in family life and what Theraplay has to offer you. The core thing to remember is that structure is all about becoming a clear, consistent, warm and playful leader for your child.

4
Engagement

In this chapter, we are going to look at what engagement means in Theraplay and why it's important. Then we'll look at why engagement sometimes becomes difficult and what we can do to re-establish it with our child using ideas from Theraplay.

What is engagement?

The element of engagement is a core part of Theraplay and is based upon what ordinary parents naturally do. In Theraplay, engagement is focused upon how we do four things:

1. We create moments of emotional connection with our child, 'now moments'.

2. We focus on her in an exclusive way, by being sensitive, soothing and delightful in our interactions with her.

3. We notice and are 'in tune' with her state.

4. We respond to our child's state so that she feels 'just right'.

Let's take a closer look at what we mean.

Emotional connection

Engagement occurs in a moment of emotional connection between a parent and child. When it is taking place, we feel fully focused on our child in a 'here and now' moment, and at the same time she feels fully focused upon us.

An emotional connection is usually a short moment when we feel 'at one' with our child and she feels connected to us. It is in this two-way moment that we are both fully focused on each other and are in harmony and sharing the joy of our companionship. During a moment of engagement, no one and nothing else seem to exist. A smile, chuckle or warm look lets us know that our child is enjoying being with us. A longer period of engagement can be made up of a collection of successive moments of connection. The key is that you both feel genuinely emotionally connected.

Exclusive focus upon your child

The exclusive focus we develop with our child usually begins early. In pregnancy, we might 'talk' to our growing baby and perhaps stroke our bump when our baby moves. We begin to notice our baby as being a unique and separate person.

Engagement

When things go well, once she is born you take delight in 'being with' each other. This two-way mutual focus and attention upon each other is where the engagement takes place. An exclusive relationship is being made. Parent and baby are often totally absorbed in each other for short periods of time and these times occur repeatedly over hours, days and weeks. The collective result of all of these moments of connection is that our child feels safe and cared for, and she associates these good feelings with us as her parent. We, as parents, build our love and adoration for our child through these moments, so that we feel a special connection with her. We often notice all the amazing things about her. What she looks like. How tiny her fingers and toes are. How lovely she is. We spend time noticing and getting to know her as a unique person. Our baby also notices us. She can hear, smell, see and feel us.

There are of course a lot of basic parenting jobs to be done, such as feeding and keeping her clean. We could get these jobs done in a task-focused way that is efficient: for instance, nappy off, wipe and then nappy back on. Job done! However, for most parents this nappy-change sequence, like many other caring tasks, becomes an opportunity for engagement. How? Well, usually you chat and play with her while the practical tasks are done. You might blow a raspberry on her tummy and she will gurgle back in delight. This nappy change has become a moment of playful connection. You seem to know just how to get her attention by using your most engaging musical sing-song voice, lively facial expressions and gestures. You also know that she needs time to pause and look away and you will naturally lower the level of excitement to give her a break. You have become 'in tune' with her and know how to respond so she feels 'just right'. Most of the time this will happen completely naturally so you might not realise all the things you are doing and how much you are helping her.

Being 'in tune' and helping her feel 'just right'

As you get to know your baby and young child, you get really good at noticing how she communicates what she is feeling in her body and mind. You learn what her different cries mean and can start to read her expressions and sounds so you know how she is. You become able to tell when she is sleepy or awake, unhappy or content. Once you are 'in tune' with her, you are then able to provide her with what she needs.

Let's look at another example, this time a typical toddler. She finds a small stone and comes to show you. You stop what you are doing and focus your attention exclusively on her, sharing her delight, with big warm eyes and a squeeze showing her that you 'get' how pleased she feels. Similarly, when she stumbles while learning to walk, you give her a soothing hug or encouraging words. You show her that you know how she is feeling and that you can help her to feel OK again. This is very calming and connecting for her. She feels known and can feel you with her.

As parents, we notice and respond when our child is overstimulated or upset. We also notice when she is bored and needs someone to play with. We move between being a comfort to also being a playmate. It's no coincidence that across the world parents sing nursery rhymes to their children. People have naturally created songs which provide ways of being playful with their babies and infants. Many nursery rhymes also provide spaces for parents and children to learn about feelings together, such as the well-known song 'This little piggy' with its themes of noticing the toes ('piggies') and then having the feeling of tension as the 'piggy' 'runs all the way home' (when parent playfully tickles his child from her toe to her tummy).

A note on tickling: Within Theraplay we take care not to tickle, but rather to be more predictable and firm in the way we touch. Tickling can seem as if it's fun but if you are not the person controlling when it will stop, it can quickly become uncomfortable.

 There is nothing better than shared moments of delight and connection with someone you love.

Engagement throughout childhood

As we all know, our child grows and her needs keep changing. She might communicate in different ways but we, as parents, develop ways to continue knowing her and be 'in synch' with her. We learn what mood she is in, when she might want our help and when to leave her to work things out. The way we show engagement may look a bit different. We might connect together over a shared meal, a joke or via a playful text message. We recognise that she needs more independence from us but still find ways to have those moments of genuine connection.

The way we engage with our children varies too between families and also cultures. Some families use a lot of humour, gentle teasing and may be quite physical together. Others create this feeling of connection in quieter ways. The exact way in which engagement happens is not important. What matters most is that our child feels that we know who she is, what matters most to her and that she is special to us. And she experiences us as being a parent who is alongside her, providing just the right type of support, at the right time.

Remember that when we think about a relationship, we are thinking about what happens between you and your child. You both bring something to how the interaction goes.

Why engagement is helpful to children: The child's perspective

From a child's perspective, the moments of connection with her parent will help her to feel valued, wanted and accepted. By having her parent focus on her, she receives the message that 'I matter' and 'I am loved and valued.' These unique interactions help her to feel that her parents accept and value her for who she is.

When her parent enjoys being with her, she learns that 'I am a good person. I am likeable.' This is how positive self-esteem and self-value get started. Also, by having her parent show empathy, she receives the message, 'I understand how you feel.' This sets the foundations for her learning to give and receive empathy.

Children of all ages thrive when they are living within environments in which they have accepting and understanding relationships. The relationships a child has, and how they feel, will lay down an expectation, or model, for how future relationships should feel. As she grows from a young child into an adolescent, she holds an understanding that a good relationship means enjoying being with someone and feeling valued and accepted. It is easy to see how this can lend itself to more successful relationships in adulthood.

Why engagement is helpful to parents: The parent's perspective

As parents, we all want to enjoy being with our children. It is important that we feel connected to our child and feel positive when we're together. These feelings provide the 'glue' of relationships and are, for many people, the very essence of what family is all about.

We also do better in other areas of our life when we have relationships with people in which we feel valued, accepted and loved. As a parent, it is hugely satisfying to have a close relationship with our child. And feeling connected with our child triggers many good-feeling chemicals in our brains, which has benefits for our whole body.

When engagement goes wrong or astray

For some children and parents, establishing a comfortable level of engagement can be difficult. This may be because of vulnerabilities in the child, the adult or often a combination of both. There are also many individual differences that have to be taken into account. We look at some different reasons below.

Why a child may find engagement difficult

There are many reasons why a child may find engagement difficult:

» Your child may be naturally quite passive or withdrawn and may need more sensitive help to be able to connect and join in with things.

» Your child may struggle with focusing her attention and may flit from one thing to another, which makes engagement hard.

» Your child may have developmental difficulties. As an example, autism spectrum disorder has, at its core, difficulties with social relationships which will make engagement especially hard for her.

» Your child may have experienced neglect during her early weeks, months or years. This meant that she missed out on early experiences of being focused upon and attended to. Now engagement doesn't feel right to her and she may try to avoid it.

It can be helpful to think about how your child responds to engagement. The child checklist may help you to reflect upon this.

Child checklist: How does your child respond to engagement?

✓ Does your child seem to stop you from getting close to her?

✓ Does your child ignore or reject you?

✓ Does your child 'act silly' when you try to get close to her or play with her?

✓ Does your child seem to get overexcited when you play together?

✓ Does your child find it difficult to attend to you when you play with her?

✓ Does your child seem too serious or find it difficult to relax and have fun?

If you answered yes to any of the questions above, then it could be useful to think about how you can start adding some Theraplay activities into family life. Some children, for whatever reason, need more help and experience with engagement.

Why parents may find engagement difficult

Parents can sometimes struggle with engagement, for a range of reasons:

» You might not feel comfortable playing and may find it hard to know how to play with your child.

» Your own experience of being parented can be important. Perhaps you had parents who were physically absent because of work, or had lots of other children to care for, and you didn't get to be with them very often. Perhaps your parents were emotionally absent, or not playful, possibly because they did not believe it was important. This might mean that you don't really know how to be engaging because you haven't experienced it yourself.

» When your child was very young, you may have been ill or had an interruption in your parenting due to hospitalisation. You may have been depressed or you may not have known how to engage with her.

» You may have experienced a difficult or life-changing event that has led to a disruption in the connection between you and your child. You may have gone through divorce, separation or bereavement. You may have changed jobs or moved house. It can be tough being a parent as we have to cope with normal life as well as take care of our family. It's natural that, at various times in our lives, stressful life events will take up our time and move our focus away from being able to connect with our child in the way we want to.

» You may currently be unwell or have difficulties which are overwhelming or distracting.

It's important to say that the levels and types of engagement in family relationships can also vary a lot. Some families are more comfortable with physical contact (such as cuddles) than others, and some use a lot more humour and lively play than others. Theraplay does not seek to make all families engage in the same way. It is not about making everyone comfortable with hugs! It simply wants to help families to feel connected and have supportive relationships with each other.

It can be helpful to think about the level and type of engagement that you provide for your child. If levels of engagement become too little, you are likely to see problems. For example, when a parent has low levels of engagement with her child for a long period of time, her child tends to become withdrawn, isolated, sad, avoidant of contact and poorly regulated. It is also possible to try to engage too much. If you are not quite 'in-tune' with your child, you may pitch your play so that she gets overexcited and out of control, or she may find it intrusive and would rather be left alone. It can be hard to get it just right.

The parent checklist provides some helpful questions to consider.

Parent checklist: What's your engagement like?

✓ Do you feel that there is too much distance between you and your child?

✓ Do you usually know what your child is feeling, or is it sometimes difficult to tell?

✓ Are you usually able to calm your child down when needed?

✓ Are you and your child able to be playful together?

✓ Do you find yourself becoming too serious or competitive when with your child?

✓ Do you find yourself trying too hard to connect with your child?

The parent checklist may have highlighted some issues for you in relation to engagement. Don't be hard on yourself. As a parent, you are doing a challenging job and it is normal to feel disconnected and overwhelmed sometimes. There are likely to be many more good moments between you and your child which you might not notice because they are brief. These small moments of connection matter.

What does engagement look like when it's present?

Here are some signs that you and your child are creating engagement together:

» You have delightful 'now' moments and genuine fun together.

» You and your child are able to be playful together whilst still getting things done.

» You are aware of your child's emotional state and you provide just what is needed.

» You are the one who is setting the emotional pace so that your child's feelings, such as excitement, do not become out of control.

» You and your child are 'in synch'.

Remember though that engagement happens in moments! Don't expect to feel completely in tune with your child for every minute of the day. Just like clouds come and go across the sky, engagement between a child and her parent switches on and off throughout the day.

It's also important to remember that it's OK for you to have times when you are not feeling playful with your child. You don't need to force yourself to be playful when you are not feeling good or relaxed yourself.

What can you do? Engagement ideas from Theraplay

There are a lot of small but important things that you can do to try and increase engagement and to develop moments of connection between you and your child.

As has already been outlined in this book, Theraplay is focused upon creating moments during the day, even if they are very brief, when you and your child are connected, having fun and feeling like you're 'in it together'.

Here are some things for you to try:

» Make a point of noticing unique things about your child, such as her freckles, hair, clothes, the way she did something. The message is, 'I am deeply interested in you, I can see you.'

» Play simple games and find small ways to have spontaneous fun. This could be an activity like hand clapping or hide and seek but can also be something like a brief shared joke, catching her eye, setting up a race, budging each other in a playful way as you walk past each other. The message is, 'We're here together and we like it.'

» Make a personal hello and goodbye part of your usual routine – in the morning, when collecting from school, when she comes in from being out. The message is, 'I missed you, I'm glad you're back' or 'See you later, I'll be thinking of you.'

» Find common interests which allow you to spend relaxed time together, like cooking, taking the dogs for a walk or watching a film.

» Make an effort to take an interest in what she is focused on, like her computer game or current craze. Listen to her enthusiasm and find out what it is she likes so much about it.

» If something hard is happening for her (even if it may seem minor to you) show deep interest and try to be alongside her. The message is, 'I can see you're not OK, I'm here and we will find a way through it.'

» Look for ways of being together where there is a feeling of a team effort. This is especially helpful if you tend to get competitive with her in an unhelpful way.

The sorts of specific activities that are helpful in practising a feeling of engagement are those which involve you focusing solely upon your child so that you can notice and respond to her. You will pay attention to special things about her and find small ways to have 'in the moment' connection with her.

Let's think about the game of Hide and Seek and why we think it's a great example of engagement.

Hide and seek

This well-known game is a more sophisticated version of Peek-a-boo. It involves a child hiding in the room, while her parent covers his eyes. The parent then finds the child and they both laugh in delight. It's fun! The parent then takes a turn at hiding. There are many variations of this game. For example, sometimes the person hiding may give clues about her whereabouts by making small animal noises as the finder gets closer to her.

This simple game plays on the idea of a parent and child separating and then finding each other again. There are many emotional aspects to this, which may not seem so obvious at first glance. The child, while hiding, will often be feeling anticipation and a building tension about being found. This feels exciting. Once found, there is a moment of positive emotion and delight which is shared. All of this creates changes in her body. A feeling of excitement during the waiting can be intense and it all ends with a shriek and a flip of the tummy when found, 'Got you!' The parent and child share and enjoy a moment of meeting and connection. This game, which is often played over and over again, gives the child experience of dealing with these intense emotions and with the repeated joy of being reunited with her parent. It also helps her practise being separated from her parent with support, a core developmental task.

Let's look now at an example of how Theraplay could help a withdrawn child.

Example: Anaya

Anaya was a quiet, withdrawn nine-year-old girl. She seemed to prefer her own company and tended to shy away from spending time with her parents. Anaya's mum tried hard to find ways to enjoy doing activities with her. Anaya enjoyed making things and doing crafts but even when her mum did these things with her, Anaya seemed to end up doing her own thing. It was as if her mum was not there. Mum was feeling confused about how they seemed to struggle to connect with each other. On the surface, it looked as though they did many things together but Mum felt that there was something missing emotionally. She wanted to find other ways to be with Anaya.

Mum tried a Theraplay approach. While doing their usual craft activity, Mum switched the focus away from the object Anaya was making to creating designs on each other instead. Mum initiated a game of decorating each other with feathers, stickers and face paints. Anaya seemed to enjoy decorating her mum and vice versa. Mum thought it might be hard for Anaya so she kept the game short, so that they were only focused on each other for a little while before they returned to decorating an object. This game became a regular part of their craft time together. Over time, Mum noticed that something seemed to be changing and their time together had become more about being together.

Ideas from Theraplay to increase engagement

Table 4.1 gives some ordinary life examples of engagement and some activities from Theraplay for you to try. Full descriptions of all of the Theraplay activities here are given in Chapter 10.

You might recognise some of the games as many are commonly seen across the world in different families. Many of the games may seem like they are for very young children because they are so simple. We have found that even older children will play 'young' games, especially when played in the privacy of their own homes, or if they have missed out on playing them at a younger age. We have included some older-child ideas too.

Table 4.1: Engagement: Ordinary life and Theraplay activities

Age	Ordinary life example of adult-led engagement	Theraplay activities to promote engagement
Infant	Greeting your baby after a nap, friendly chat during dressing, rocking your baby, developing daily routines of wake–feed–sleep, holding your baby	Peek-a-boo; Beep and honk; Pop cheeks; Hello, goodbye
Toddler	Involving them with everyday activities in a playful way (being your helper), noticing how they are growing and all the things they can do, singing and playing games that involve changes in pace and surprise	This little pig went to market; Row, row, row your boat; Piggy-back/ Horsey-back ride; Hide and seek; Blow me over

Primary age	Sharing experiences such as having a meal together, playing at the park, greeting child after school, having fun together	Check-ups; Variations of hide and seek; hand-clapping games; Foil prints; Sticker match; Create a special hand-shake; Copy funny faces; Push-me-over, pull-me-up; Decorate each other with feathers, stickers and face paints
Teen	Staying in touch during the day via phone calls, texts, SMS, noticing their clothes and changing styles, sharing jokes, spending relaxed time together	Mirroring; Copy funny faces; Create rhythms with cups; Make up a rap; Foil prints; Manicure; Cotton ball hockey or Ping-pong ball with straws

Summing up

In this chapter, we have looked at what engagement is from a Theraplay perspective and why it's important for our children and for us as parents. We have looked at what can sometimes get in the way of engagement and have shared some ideas from Theraplay to help us to re-find it.

The core thing to remember is that engagement is all about feeling connected with, and 'in tune' with, your child for some brief moments during each day.

5

Nurture

In this chapter, we look at how nurture is described in Theraplay and why it's important for our children and us as parents. Then we look at why it sometimes goes astray and what we can do to re-establish it with our child using ideas from Theraplay.

What is nurture?

The element of nurture is a core part of Theraplay and is based upon what ordinary parents naturally do. In Theraplay, nurture is focused upon how we do three things:

1. We take care of our child so that he feels cared for and valued.

2. We interact with our child in ways that are soothing, calming and reassuring.

3. We make the world feel safe and predictable for our child.

Let's look at this more deeply.

Caring for your child so he feels cared for and valued

When you look after your young baby, you do many nurturing things for him, including feeding, changing his nappy, cuddling, rocking and comforting him when he cries. These nurturing tasks often involve actions which meet his essential physical needs. They are also emotional too. When you feed your baby for example, you are not only meeting his physical need for food, you are also giving him an emotional message that reassures him and says, 'It's my job to look after you' and 'I know just what you need right now.' In fact, all these caring tasks give him the message that you will look after him. He grows up knowing that you will meet his needs and the world feels safe.

As a parent, you also think ahead for your child by trying to anticipate what he will need next so that you are ready to attend to, and comfort him, when he needs this. Just consider the sheer amount of planning that goes into packing your baby's bag for a day out: bottles, nappies, spare clothes and maybe a small toy! As his parent, you try to think of all of his possible needs. This means that when your baby cries later on, you can swiftly respond. This sequence of you being prepared, you hearing your baby signal that he needs something and you then satisfying his need, occurs over and over again, day after day. By doing so, you give him the message that 'I understand and know what you need. I'm ready.'

Interact in ways that are soothing, calming and reassuring

While caring for his many needs, you also respond to your child in ways that are soothing, calming and reassuring. If you were to watch a parent with her baby, you would see the parent using many different ways of soothing her baby when he is distressed. This can include rocking him, singing to him, holding him and maybe stroking his back gently. These combinations of calm words and gentle touch help her baby to feel held and supported.

Make the world feel safe and predictable

By being a constant provider of care and comfort for your child, you make his world feel safe. In fact, for a baby, you are his whole world. He is not yet aware of the world that exists beyond his relationship with you. By making his world with you feel safe and predictable, you help him become ready to explore the bigger world.

Nurture throughout childhood

As your child grows older, the kinds of nurture he needs from you will gradually change. Your toddler learns to walk and run. He will inevitably fall and accidentally bump himself, but by being ready with a comforting hug, he copes better with these accidents. He knows that you are ready to reassure and calm him when the world feels threatening.

By the time he is a school-aged child, he will have learnt to do many things for himself. You don't need to provide as much physical nurture as you did when he was younger. He still needs some comfort and reassurance from you but you offer this in a different way and it may seem less obvious. You may wash his hair and style it. You may enjoy clothes shopping with him and talking with him about things that matter to him. You may sit and enjoy a film together and share some snacks. He still needs emotional nurture from you. You may notice when he seems worried or unhappy and talk about it with him, or you may show you care by running a warm bath for him. Through all of these activities, you are letting him know, often without words, that you understand him, are available to him and you know what he needs.

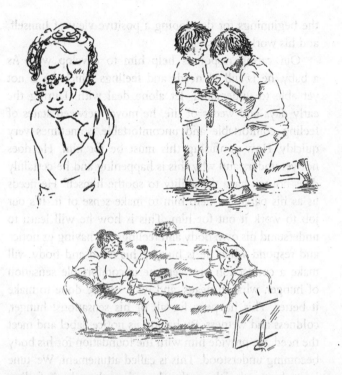

Why nurture is helpful to children:
The child's perspective

When your baby is born, he is obviously completely
dependent upon you for all of his needs, from food to
warmth. The early days and weeks are spent by you being
focused upon meeting his needs. These repeated moments
of noticing and responding give him the experience that
you will think about him, understand him and be ready
to provide him with comfort, care, affection and help. He
grows up knowing that people will look after him. When
you offer him kind and gentle care, you send the unsaid
message that he is 'wanted', 'loveable' and that 'good things
happen to him'. Every care-taking action from you is a
message of love, acceptance and worthiness. This gives him

the beginnings for developing a positive view of himself, and his world feels safe.

Our caring responses help him to develop well. As a baby, he is full of needs and feelings which he is not yet able to understand, let alone deal with. During the early days and weeks of life, he moves between states of feeling comfortable and uncomfortable, sometimes very quickly. How confusing this must be for him. He does not yet understand why this is happening and he certainly does not yet have the ability to soothe himself. He needs us as his parent to help him to make sense of it. It's our job to work it out for him. This is how he will learn to understand his own body and feelings. By having us notice and respond when he is hungry, his mind and body will make a connection between the uncomfortable sensation of hunger, what it means, and what can be done to make it better. This happens for all of his sensations: hunger, coldness and wetness. By having us notice, label and meet the need, we provide him with the foundation for his body becoming understood. This is called attunement. We 'tune in' to him and pick up the clues about how he is feeling and what he might need. He takes in the care that we give him and can feel it, and as he does this, he becomes more able to soothe himself as he grows.

 Providing care and soothing helps your child feel wanted, loved and safe.

So, the nurture we give to him helps him to learn about his body. Nurture also helps him to understand his emotions. We comfort him when he cries. We laugh with him when he does something cute and funny. He learns what feelings are and that you have feelings too.

We also use nurture to help calm our child. As a young toddler, when he is upset about a lost toy, we might scoop him up and provide him with a calm hug. Often the nurture we offer includes different types of kind touch. Physical touch from us can help him to calm down and become more regulated. Research has found that children who experience a lot of physical nurture tend to be calmer. Conversely, children who experience little positive touch can become more overactive. We spoke more about touch in Chapter 2.

Why nurture is helpful to parents: The parent's perspective

Once we become parents we have an in-built drive which makes us want to protect and care for our children. Some might say that our job as a parent is to ensure that our offspring survive. We need to keep our species going!

It's hard work looking after our children but it can also be rewarding. Many parents will recall the difficult process of trying to work out exactly what your baby needs when he cries. Is he hungry, wet or bored? It can feel hugely satisfying when we finally work out how to soothe him.

When things go well, we get very good at attuning to our child's emotions and needs. This makes it possible for us to notice and respond to the smallest sign of distress or discomfort in our child. Once you have got to know each other well, you will know when 'he's not quite right'. The pleasure and reward of experiencing closeness with your child can be very strong. It feels good to feel close and emotionally connected.

When nurture goes wrong or astray
For some children and parents, establishing a comfortable level of nurture is difficult. Let's look at some reasons for this.

Why a child may find nurture difficult
Children may find nurture difficult for many different reasons:

» Some children find the physical aspects of nurture difficult to cope with (see Chapter 2 for more discussion about touch).

» There are individual differences between babies and children. Some really enjoy cuddles and being held while others are much more sensitive and get upset if handled too much. Some babies and children are much harder to soothe than others.

» Your child may have a developmental condition such as autism spectrum disorder or sensory processing difficulties which can make him particularly sensitive to physical touch.

» Your child may have had experiences of painful and confusing medical procedures which now make receiving care through touch very difficult. He might react to your touch as if it is painful.

» Your child may have been premature and has difficulties with touch.

» If your child doesn't like being rocked or lifted off the ground it could be that he has sensory difficulties with movement.

There might be something that has happened in your child's early months that makes nurture hard for him. For instance:

» Your child may not have experienced sensitive care in his early years. Maybe his parent couldn't pick up on his feelings and needs or couldn't meet his needs. This might be for many reasons. His parents may have had mental health difficulties or been unable to look after themselves or been living in very stressful conditions. Whatever the reason, your child hasn't experienced much sensitive care and your care will be new to him so he may find it difficult. He has learned to cope on his own (even if he was very young) and this may feel more comfortable for him now. This could mean that he acts 'as if' he is older than he really is.

» If your child has experienced abusive kinds of touch, then this will lead to him learning that touch (even kind and safe touch) is something to be wary of.

» Your child may have been neglected and not touched enough. Your child may have been left to manage feelings and sensations alone, and now when you try to nurture him he pulls away.

» There may also be difficulties with nurture that may not directly relate to touch. For instance, the feeling of being cared for may feel alien. Or it may feel frightening to him to feel understood or close to someone else if he is used to being on his own. A close connection with another person can feel scary even without touch.

For many different reasons, your child may not have learned that nurture can be helpful and good for him. We have noticed that children who have had poor experiences of nurture can often become overactive, aggressive or act too mature for their age. It might not seem as if this is a difficulty with accepting nurture, but very often, if you increase the amount of nurture or kind touch you are giving him, then the aggression or overactivity goes down. Other children show very young emotional behaviour while others can become very clingy. But although they are seeking some soothing from you, it doesn't seem to help when you provide it.

All of these difficulties are very hard for you as the parent, as well as for your child. You want him to know that he can rely on you to help him feel comforted and safe. You want him to experience the calming effects of touch and warm emotional care. The nurture activities that we use within Theraplay can help you to provide this experience but they need to be used sensitively and adapted to your child, so that he may begin to feel more comfortable with the experience.

It can be helpful to think about how your child responds to nurture. The child checklist may help you to think about this.

Child checklist: How does your child respond to nurture?

- ✓ Does your child seem to avoid letting you comfort him?
- ✓ Does your child accept nurturing touch from you?
- ✓ Does your child try to take care of his own needs?
- ✓ Is your child overly clingy with you?
- ✓ Does your child seem to reject you?

✓ Is your child able to soothe himself?

✓ Is your child easy or hard to calm down when distressed?

✓ Does your child physically move away when you try to care for him?

✓ Is your child reluctant to share emotions of sadness, anger or hurt?

Your responses to the checklist may have highlighted some issues regarding how your child responds to nurture from you. For whatever reason, your child may need more experience with receiving nurture. Your child may have missed out on good experiences of nurture when he was younger or you may feel that some extra nurture at this stage may be really helpful. When life is busy and stressful then nurture can often get missed for a time. You can always go back and fill in the gaps. Theraplay has some ideas for meeting some of your child's need for nurture.

Why parents may find nurture difficult

There are a lot of individual and cultural differences around touch and nurture and the important part is that the nurture feels right for your family.

Parents can sometimes find offering nurture to their child difficult for many reasons:

» You may be someone who is not very comfortable with touch.

» Your own experience of being cared for when you were small is important in helping you learn how to nurture your child. Maybe your parents didn't provide much touch or nurture. Parents used to be advised not to touch their children so they might have followed this advice thinking they were doing the right thing. We now know that children really need touch and nurture. If you had difficult experiences of touch and nurture yourself then it can be useful to spend some time thinking about your childhood and to become more aware of how it is influencing the way you are with your child. Were your parents cuddly and physically affectionate? Did they notice when you felt unhappy? What did they do to comfort you? How did you learn about managing difficult feelings?

» If you had difficulties yourself when your child was small, then you might not have been able to be calm and available for him, and this might make him reluctant to relax and let himself be looked after now.

» Other difficult things may have happened in your life, like divorce, bereavement or illness, which meant there were times when you had too much to cope with yourself.

From time to time, it can be difficult for all of us to be nurturing to our children. Sometimes we are exhausted and stressed, which can then make it difficult for us to be able to offer nurture to our child. Maybe you are in need of some nurture yourself. Remember the safety advice we are given on aeroplanes: 'Put on your own oxygen mask before you look after your child.' This is very true. We would encourage you to look after yourself and make sure that you are cared for by your friends and the adults in your family.

It's much easier to provide nurture to your child when you also feel cared for.

Another possible difficulty is that you may be providing nurture but perhaps it is out of tune with your child's needs for nurture. For instance, you may have become too focused on discipline and do not pick up the signs that he needs more nurture, or perhaps you really want to nurture him but it is for your own comfort rather than when he needs it. Adding more nurture which is really focused on what your child needs, and can manage, can really make a difference.

It can be helpful to think about the level and type of nurture that you provide to your child. The parent checklist has some questions for you to consider.

Parent checklist: What's your nurture like?

✓ Do you feel comfortable with physical affection, such as cuddling your child?

✓ Can you tell when your child is becoming tense, distressed and in need of being calmed?

✓ Do you have a variety of ways to soothe and calm your child when he is distressed or tense?

✓ Is it easy or difficult to soothe your child?

✓ How do you show nurture to your child?

✓ Do you feel in a rush to make your child's hurt feelings go away?

The checklist above may have highlighted some issues for you in relation to nurture. Remember that it's not possible to provide nurture for your child all the time and, for you to be able to do this, you need to feel supported yourself. Concentrate on building small moments of nurture and being realistic. If your child is very sensitive, it will be a lot harder and you will need support to keep trying.

What does nurture look like when it's present?

Here are some signs that you and your child are creating nurture together:

» You provide nurturing contact (such as touch, calm words and care) to your child, which he accepts.

» You and your child have moments of calmness together when you are able to take care of a need.

» You are able to soothe your child when he is distressed.

» Your child can come to you when he has a stressful problem without fearing that you will become angry, judgemental or that you will begin to lecture him or try to quickly reassure him.

What can you do? Nurture ideas from Theraplay

There are many simple things that you can try which will add more nurture into your daily life with your child.

Nurture is about finding moments:

» to give your child a loving hug or cuddle.

» to notice when your child is distressed, express concern for him and comfort him.

» to have moments when you connect with empathy.

» to take care of your child in ways that convey the message, 'It's my job to take care of you.'

Here are some things for you to try:

» Put your arm around your child when you are together doing an everyday activity, such as watching TV.

» Give your child a hand or back massage.

» Use face paints to decorate and paint your child.

» Use different snacks to feed your child and notice what he likes and doesn't like.

» Draw around your child's hand on a piece of paper and then decorate the drawing together.

» Pretend to tell your child's fortune using his hand.

» Sing to your child. You could change the words of popular songs so they become about your child in a loving and kind way.

The sorts of specific activities that are helpful in practising a feeling of nurture often involve some kind of physical touch.

Let's look at an example from Theraplay.

Caring for hurts

Why would an activity called 'Caring for hurts' be helpful? This activity involves sitting with your child while you gently apply lotion to his hands and arms. While applying the lotion, you notice and care for any scratches, bruises or hurts. You notice these 'hurts' by putting lotion around them. You don't need to say any words. It's the action that counts. By doing this, your child sees that you are noticing these 'hurts' and he feels you taking care of him.

An alternative with an older child might be to look at his hand (while you hold it in yours) and then notice if you can see any letters or pictures in the lines of his hand. You could add a small amount of talcum powder to make the lines stand out. Through the activity, you can provide some caring touch and a feeling of closeness without awkwardness as your child is concentrating on looking at the patterns in his hand.

In Theraplay we think about how we might use games to provide opportunities for us to nurture and calm our child. And we try to introduce calming touch in ways that feel natural. Let's look at an example of how Theraplay could help to calm an 'on-the-go', energetic child.

Example: Mo

Mo was a lively, energetic five-year-old. From the moment she was awake in the morning, she was on the go. Mum found it exhausting to keep up with her. Mum filled the day with activities that kept Mo busy in the hope that it would tire Mo out and they would then be able to have a moment of quiet and calm at the end of the day. That rarely happened and bedtimes had become loud and disorganised.

Mum took a Theraplay approach. She began to find opportunities when she could offer small moments of nurture to Mo. In the morning, while making breakfast, Mum sang a gentle song about Mo that Mo could overhear. While eating together, Mum playfully fed Mo some of her food. At bedtime, Mum applied lotion to Mo's arms and legs in a calm and gentle manner. She added a gentle song. This became a nightly ritual which gave both of them a moment of calmness together. Gradually Mo started to relax. They both began to enjoy spending this close time together.

Ideas from Theraplay to increase nurture

Table 5.1 provides some examples of nurture activities that are commonly seen in everyday life. We have also added in some Theraplay activities for you to try. As with the activities given for the previous dimensions, you might recognise some of the games. You don't need to do these activities exactly as they are described. It's OK to make up your own. The main aim is to think about how you can give your child the message through action and experience, rather than words, that you are there to care for him.

Table 5.1: Nurture: Ordinary life and Theraplay activities

Age	Ordinary life example of adult-led nurture	Theraplay activities to promote nurture
Infant	Feeding, changing nappies, bathing and rocking	Feeding; Lullaby; Rocking; Special kisses (with parent)
Toddler	Bath-time, towelling dry, feeding with a spoon, providing calm bedtime routine (stories)	Caring for hurts; Slippery, slippery, slip; Personalised twinkle song
Primary age	Singing with your child, lotion child after bath-time, playing 'dress-up', styling child's hair	Decorate child; Feather match; Face painting; Pass a squeeze; Pizza massage; Blanket swing
Teen	Giving your child a manicure, styling hair, shopping for clothes together, giving a foot massage, sitting watching an enjoyable film together, sharing snacks	Lotion or powder prints; Playful snack sharing (Doughnut challenge); Temporary tattoos; Trace messages; Weather report

Summing up

This chapter has focused upon what nurture is from a Theraplay perspective and why it is important for our child and for us as parents. We have thought about why nurture sometimes goes astray in family life and what Theraplay has to offer us.

The core thing to remember is that nurture is all about finding moments when you can offer calm, soothing and quiet care to your child at opportune or planned moments throughout the day.

6
Challenge

In this chapter, we look at what challenge means in Theraplay, why it's important and why it can sometimes become difficult. We then look at what you can do to add challenge into your interactions with your child, using ideas from Theraplay.

What is challenge?

The element of challenge is a core part of Theraplay and is based on what ordinary parents do. In Theraplay, challenge is focused on how we do three things:

1. We support our child's natural instincts to explore the world (having established a secure base).

2. We support our child in doing activities she is ready to do, while also extending her skills a little bit. We want to support her development and growth and her sense of competence.

3. We help our child to manage experiences that give her the feeling of tension.

Let's explain this in a bit more detail.

Supporting her instinct to explore
Children naturally want to explore and play. When you provide a secure emotional base and a stimulating

environment, your child will instinctively go off to explore and will learn about relationships and the world around her. As her parent, your role is to help her to feel safe enough to leave you. You also judge what is the right level of support that she needs from you, so that she can relax and play. All children are unique and may need different levels of support. There are also differences between parents of course. Some parents find it very easy to let their child go, whereas others may find they want to keep their child close. All of these things will affect how her exploration develops.

Supporting her to do activities she can do, while also extending her skills

Children change fast from the moment they are born. As a parent, you will recognise the many changes that your baby makes in her development by the time she is one year old. In the space of a year, she learns to sit, crawl and walk, and she begins to talk. It is amazing the sheer number of skills your young infant acquires in a short period of time.

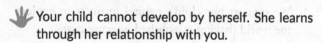 Your child cannot develop by herself. She learns through her relationship with you.

Watch any parent with his child and you will observe him encouraging his infant to develop to her next developmental step. He may hold her and encourage her to walk, clapping and smiling as she tries. He may give her a spoon to hold while he feeds her, in preparation for her learning to feed herself.

The key idea here is that you encourage and gently challenge your child towards taking the next step in her development. Your expectations are realistic and you set up activities that can engage her just at the point before it becomes too difficult, so that she can succeed and move forward just a little. When she succeeds, you share in her delight. This gives her a feeling of mastery and competence, 'I can do it.' She can feel your pride in her – 'You think I'm great' – and she builds confidence that you will be there when she needs help.

You also help her understand and manage the difficult feelings or tension that arise for her as she learns a new skill. For example, your toddler who is practising the art of balancing on two feet may need a steadying hand and a warm hug from you when she topples over. As a parent, you encourage her to develop abilities and competence while being a source of support. This means that she can learn all about her body and what it can do, while also learning about emotion.

Managing experiences that feel tense

Within the challenge dimension in Theraplay, we are also interested in how you help your child to cope in situations which have different levels of arousal. By arousal, we mean the excitement, tension and stimulation that she feels. When things go well your child will learn how to deal with different levels of excitement and many different situations. This learning usually begins at a very early age, during babyhood. Let's look at an example by exploring the simple game of Peek-a-boo.

Peek-a-boo

This game involves you hiding your face from your infant or toddler. You then re-appear by moving your hands away. When you are hidden, your baby will feel some tension ('Where have you gone?'). Then there is surprise and delight when you re-appear. This is such a simple game but it actually involves quite complex emotions for your baby, particularly as her emotions change quite quickly from tension to delight. By playing this game over and over again, you help her learn to manage strong feelings.

Challenge throughout childhood

As your child grows older, you continue to guide and support her along the path of learning new skills. This goes well when you encourage her to learn skills that build upon what she can already do, without making the steps too big. She learns best when she begins from a place of mastery. For example, when your toddler has mastered walking, she might next be encouraged to sit on a tricycle, but you would not encourage her to ride a bike without stabilisers. You present your child with opportunities to develop her next skill, which fits with what she is currently able to do. There are no huge jumps! This provides her with realistic expectations about what she can manage and builds in success for her. This is the same for older children. You support her to build upon skills she already has.

At times of stress, your child may be less able to do things than when she is relaxed. You will naturally reduce the level of challenge and expectation of what she can manage, and increase it again when she is ready.

Why challenge is helpful to children: The child's perspective

All children have a natural desire and urge to develop and grow. Your child's body and mind are primed for growth, and with the right level of support she will naturally learn. When she knows that you will protect her from harm, she will feel more confident to try new things. When you help her understand and manage difficult feelings, such as frustration, tension and excitement, then she will begin to learn how to manage these feelings by herself. When you know just what she is ready to learn next, and provide support for her to succeed, she will develop a sense of her own competence.

Over time, she develops confidence in her own ability to do things and to make an impact on her world. This is the foundation for independence. She develops a firm belief about herself, 'I can do things', which is the seed for later self-confidence.

As a parent, you will usually enjoy being with your child as she grows and develops skills. You smile when she first smiles and you take delight in each new step she takes. She absorbs your enjoyment of her and takes these positive feelings inside herself. For her, these repeated experiences of having you lovingly encourage, support and enjoy her tiny successes, gives her confidence in her own ability to learn and develop.

Within the challenge dimension, you are giving your child the message, 'You are capable of growing and of making a positive impact on the world' and 'I will support you.'

Why challenge is helpful to parents:
The parent's perspective

Parenting comes with the hope that you will help your child to become a strong, independent and capable adult. As parents, we often feel a huge sense of satisfaction when our child is able to do something. Just consider the delight you feel when your child takes her first independent steps and walks across the room. It is so rewarding to see her becoming confident in her own abilities and body. This sense of pride continues as she grows. We work hard to support her and celebrate in her successes. Watching her develop over the years gives us the sense that we are doing a good job with parenting.

When challenge goes wrong or astray

For some children and parents, establishing a comfortable level of challenge is difficult. Some of the reasons for this are similar to those we outlined in the previous dimension chapters.

Why a child may find challenge difficult

Children may find challenge difficult for a variety of reasons:

» Your child may be anxious, shy and reluctant to try new activities. Children have different temperaments, which means that they need different kinds of physical and emotional support. Children also learn at very different rates.

» Your child may have had a difficult start to her life which meant that she missed out on opportunities to practise and learn new things. If your child lacks confidence in herself then she may not want to risk failure.

» Your child may have been cared for by adults who were unable to support her enough. Different things may have happened in the past which make new learning and exploration hard for her, especially if she is fearful of failing. Perhaps she has not had opportunities to learn (for example, no one played with her), or the support was not at the right level (for example, she was expected to do things she wasn't ready for yet), or perhaps she was laughed at or punished when she got things wrong. All of these situations might lead to her being reluctant to try new things now.

» Your child may be over-competitive. It is worth knowing that many children tend to be competitive, particularly during their primary school years, but if competitiveness becomes too strong then it may stop your child from taking the risk of losing.

So, for many different reasons, your child may find new activities difficult and she may struggle to feel successful. She may need lots of experience of being successful with the same activity before she is ready to move on to trying something new. On the other hand, she may seem to be more outgoing and may throw herself into activities which she is not yet ready for. She may need you to reign in her enthusiasm a little so that the activities stay safe and within her capability. It is also hard when your child is at a different developmental stage to her friends and everyone expects her to be able to do what they can do.

It can be helpful to think about how your child responds to challenge. The child checklist has some things for you to consider.

Child checklist: How does your child respond to challenge?

- ✓ Does your child avoid or seem anxious when trying something new, even when it's really simple?

- ✓ Does she seem to always need to get things right or perfect?

- ✓ Does she cope well with frustration?

- ✓ Does she take risks? Can she slow down when things become too hard?

- ✓ Can she allow you to help her when she is finding things hard?

✓ Does she say she 'can't do' things immediately, or the opposite, that she is the best, the fastest and knows everything?

Your answers to the checklist may have got you thinking about how your child copes with challenge. Theraplay has some ideas for how you can practise challenge with your child.

Why parents may find challenge difficult

Parents can sometimes struggle with challenge for different reasons:

» You might find it tricky to know what to expect from your child's development and how to help her learn how to do things. You may not know what to expect as your child grows up, perhaps because you haven't spent much time with very young children. You may be unknowingly trying to encourage your child to practise a skill which her body and mind are just not ready for. It can be similar to trying to get a toddler straight onto a bike without stabilisers.

» Your child may have uneven development so that she can do some things well but not other things. For example, some children are really good at school work but find sharing or relationships very hard. This makes it hard for you to predict what she will be able to cope with and you may make mistakes in your expectations.

» Your child may have experienced an illness or have a disability which has made it difficult for you to gauge where she is in terms of developing skills and confidence in different activities. You may have become overprotective of your child.

» If you are an adoptive parent, you may have begun to parent your child at an older age, which has meant that you didn't get the opportunity to see how she has developed over time. It may also be harder to see signs of her getting stressed and needing help as she might give the impression that she can cope on her own.

» You may have developed a style of being competitive with your child. While this may be useful in some situations, too much competitiveness could lead to your child losing confidence in her own abilities. It could also add stress to your relationship.

» Your own experiences of being parented can have a big influence on how you approach things. For instance, your parents may have really valued achievement and this makes you push your child.

Parents have often asked us questions such as, 'Why does my child get so stressed when other children seem to be able to cope?' or 'Why does my child have a meltdown when she tries to do something really simple?' These are common difficulties when children find new learning difficult. They become stressed when faced with something unfamiliar and this often makes things worse. Add on adult pressure or disappointment and things can quickly unravel.

The parent checklist provides some helpful questions for you to consider.

Parent checklist: What's your challenge like?

✓ Do you sometimes find it difficult knowing what your child can and cannot do?

✓ Does your child find it difficult to handle frustration? Can you find ways to help her?

✓ Do you find yourself being competitive or expecting too much of your child?

✓ Do you find it easy or hard to teach your child new things?

✓ Do you avoid challenging her because you worry about her reaction?

✓ Do you think you sometimes expect too much of her?

✓ Does your child seem very sensitive to failure? Are you able to find ways to help her try?

The checklist above may have highlighted some issues for you in relation to challenge. Let's move on and think about how Theraplay can help you to develop this dimension.

What does challenge look like when it's present?

Here are some signs that you and your child have developed helpful moments of challenge:

» You can understand your child's abilities and the things she finds hard. You are usually able to predict the sorts of things and times when your child may need more support from you.

» You are good at knowing when your child begins to feel stressed and can find ways to help her.

» You can provide enough support for her so that she can focus and attend and have a feeling of something going well.

» You are able to make tasks fit 'just right' by choosing something your child can do, and only adding in a little bit of newness (which you know she can do).

» You take pleasure in your child when she makes small steps, whether this is in doing an activity or learning something new in her relationship with you.

Challenge is about focusing upon what your child can comfortably do, and adding in something very tiny for her to try next. Your child wants and needs to feel successful. Remember that challenge applies to emotional development too. It may be that, for your child, being able to have some moments of 'to and fro' with you or being able to share a smile will be the most important steps.

What can you do? Challenge ideas from Theraplay

There are a lot of small but important things that you can do to give your child the feeling of success and gently support her growth, development and sense of competence.

Challenge is about finding moments for you to:

» give your child new experiences of feeling success.

» find ways to support her which give her the confidence to try, for example, by breaking tasks down or by doing it with her.

» give your child a sense of mastery by encouraging her to do tasks that you know she can do – succeeding will give her confidence.

» provide opportunities for her to try new things (when you feel sure that she is ready) at a gradual pace which build upon her existing skills – you try to provide emotional and practical support before she becomes frustrated.

Note. When your child finds it hard to try new things, it is tempting to concentrate on this area and to try to help her learn. Parents often say, 'I want to build her confidence so we are doing some hard activities to show her she can do it.' Be careful because this may put her under more pressure. It is usually a better idea to reduce your expectations and keep challenge very low, and to concentrate on the other three dimensions so that she feels secure and cared for before you try to introduce more challenge.

Parents can also stop their children exploring because they are feeling overprotective. In this situation, it is useful to ask yourself whether there may be ways to help yourself feel calmer so that you can let your child have a bit more freedom to explore.

Here are some Theraplay ideas for you to try:

» Choose an activity that your child can already do and change it slightly. For example, if your child is able to stand tall and still, have her next try balancing cushions on her head.

» Play games which involve the two of you doing something slightly difficult together, such as three-legged walking. You make the activity manageable by doing it as a team.

» Choose activities in which your child can easily achieve success. This is important for her to develop a feeling of mastery – 'I can do it.' Celebrate when it goes well.

The sorts of specific activities that are helpful in practising a feeling of competence are those which begin with something your child can already do, but then add some slight difficulty or tension.

Let's look at an example from Theraplay.

Balancing

Why would a Balancing game be helpful? In Theraplay, one example of a Balancing game involves a child standing on a cushion. The parent helps her to balance by holding her safely. Once this is mastered, additional cushions are then added one at a time for as long as she is enjoying the game and is successful. The parent places one cushion at a time on the pile and the child balances on the tower of pillows. Variations on this game could involve, for instance, balancing books on her head and then walking across the room. The important part is that the parent provides actual physical and emotional support to make sure it is achievable. These balancing games involve the child having to use her body to do something quite complex, while being supported to do so by her parent. When the activity is just hard enough and just the right amount of help is provided, she will feel pleased and proud of herself. She experiences a surge of good feelings when she realises she is able to do it.

Let's look at an example of how Theraplay could help a competitive child.

Example: Jed

Jed was an eight-year-old boy who liked to win when he played games with his parents. It is typical for children to be intensely competitive at this age but Jed's parents were finding his competitiveness difficult to deal with. The family avoided playing games because Jed had a complete angry meltdown if he did not win. Jed's parents were finding it more and more difficult to enjoy activities with him. He also seemed to get bored easily, which led to his parents running out of ideas about what to do with him.

Dad tried a Theraplay approach. He realised that most eight-year-olds are competitive and are poor losers. He thought about games they could play that were not stressful competitive games. Jed's dad began to play simple cooperative games with him for brief moments whenever the opportunity arose. For example, while sitting at the kitchen table, Dad playfully blew a cotton ball across the table to Jed. Jed couldn't resist blowing it back and, before they knew it, they were enjoying a brief game of 'blow the cotton ball back and forth'. Dad was careful to play this game for a short time before it got too competitive and also resisted telling Jed that he was doing well. He didn't want to spark off an outburst of 'I'm better than you.' Instead, Dad focused just on getting a 'back and forth' blowing rhythm with Jed and enjoyed being with his son.

The challenge dimension of Theraplay can also be used to draw out children who are anxious. Let's have a look at an example.

Example: Nadia

Nadia was a withdrawn and anxious nine-year-old. She often refused to try new things. This was frustrating for her dad who knew that Nadia was physically able to do the things requested of her. It seemed that Nadia could not cope emotionally with new challenges. Nadia's dad felt as though he was spending each day trying to coax her to do things.

Nadia's dad decided on a Theraplay approach. Nadia loved bubbles so her dad began to play a game of 'Pop the bubble'. At first Dad told Nadia to simply 'pop the bubble'. Then he changed the game so that he blew a bubble, which Nadia then blew back to him. Dad and Nadia together took turns to blow the bubble back and forth for as long as possible before it popped. Nadia was so engrossed with the bubbles that she didn't realise that she was learning to cope with a new activity.

Ideas from Theraplay to increase challenge

Table 6.1 gives some ordinary life examples of challenge and some activities from Theraplay for you to try.

Table 6.1: Challenge: Ordinary life and Theraplay activities

Age	Ordinary life example of adult-led challenge	Theraplay activity to promote challenge
Infant	Copying games with your face and voice, gently moving her and bouncing her on a lap, encouraging her to sit or to crawl to you	Wriggle in and out of arms
Toddler	Supporting her while she learns to walk, playing jumping or climbing games, holding her hand while she balances or walks along a short wall, helping her push her toy	Crawling race; Jump-start-stop; Pillow push; Tug-of-war
Primary age	Holding her bicycle while she learns to ride, helping her down when she has gone too high, encouraging her when she tries new things	Balancing activities; Balance on pillows; Jump off; Feather blow/grab; Straight face challenge; Balloon balance; Karate chop
Teen	Supporting her in her hobbies and celebrating effort and success, noticing when she is finding something hard and finding ways to make the task more achievable for her	Balloon tennis; Cotton ball hockey; Pick up objects with toes; Cotton ball ping-pong; Balancing challenges, Newspaper flick-toss; Cooperative races; Thumb wrestle; Tug-of-war; Arm wrestling; Seed spitting contest

Summing up

In this chapter, we have looked at what challenge is from a Theraplay perspective and why it is important in family life. We have looked at why children and parents may find challenge difficult and have outlined some ideas from

Theraplay for finding ways to help your child cope with and enjoy challenge.

The core thing to remember is that challenge is about your child experiencing success and mastery, with you being there to help them and to share in their delight.

Part 2

Everyday
Examples

7

Using Theraplay to Help with Everyday Transitions and Change

Every day we face different transitions – for instance, waking up and getting out of bed, starting and stopping activities and getting to and from places. Negotiating these daily transitions can be difficult at times and, as parents, it is these moments that are often the trickiest parts of the day. Why is this?

We all know that major changes such as moving house or school, the end of a relationship, a bereavement, or a change in health can be very stressful, but even small everyday transitions involve some stress. Each transition involves shifting from one thing to another. This might mean a change in physiological or emotional state, or a move from one place to another. This shift can be difficult. In order to move onto the next thing (for example, getting up in the morning), you have to let go of the thing before (for example, being cosy in bed). You also have to organise yourself while staying calm enough to make the shift smoothly. All of this takes a complicated combination of skills. When your child is young, he needs you to organise things so that he can stay calm and relaxed. As he gets older he will start to get better at doing this for himself, but even then, the changes we face every day are often hard.

Exercise: Think for a moment

» Think about all the things you do in a day to help you manage ordinary transitions. Do you have a set morning or bedtime routine to help you? Do you have a particular way you get dressed or tidy away? What would happen if someone messed up your usual system or removed your toothbrush? Would you become agitated and tense? What would you do to cope?

» Think about what you do when you start to become stressed. Let's say someone has driven aggressively and pulled in front of you, how do you feel and what do you do to try and calm yourself? Let's say you're out with friends messing around and things start to feel a bit out of hand. How do you notice and what might you do?

Without knowing it, all of us set up rituals and patterns in the way we do things, in order to help ourselves get through these everyday challenges. When things go wrong, for instance we can't find our car keys or there is a missing PE kit, we often become tense and more likely to get into an argument. The same is true for our children.

How can Theraplay help?

Theraplay ideas can be used in many everyday situations to support children through transitions. Theraplay can also help us and our children spot trigger points and see more clearly when things start to go wrong. If your child is vulnerable, then he may need extra sensitivity and support to help him through transitions. If your child becomes stressed and anxious at transition points, he may suddenly behave in a younger, more awkward way than usual.

It's important that you realise that these are hard moments for your child. Like reinforcing a vulnerable building, you can put in extra support and lower your expectations about what he will be able to manage. Here are some ideas about moving from one place to another and also about the changes in your body (for example, from feeling calm to excited and back again), so that your child can stay within a comfortable level of excitement.

Getting from one place to another

Moving from one place to another – for example, from the house to the car, from the TV to the bathroom – or managing a longish walk can easily turn into battles between you.

Try turning the movement into some kind of activity or game so that the journey itself can become enjoyable. He might forget to battle, get involved in the activity, and the end point is that he has got to where you want him to be (without him quite realising that that was your purpose).

Some ideas
Do something as a team

» Balance a cushion between you, balance something on your head or walk three legged.

» Think of funny ways to cross the room like being an animal, put his feet on top of your feet, hop together.

» Do a wheelbarrow (where you hold his legs while he walks on his hands).

» See if you can stand up and sit down by holding each other's arms, or back to back, or see if you are strong enough to pull him up.

Change the pace and use rhythm

» While walking, move from slow to fast, stop and start. Rhymes and small songs work well, for example, singing, 'One, two, three, wheeee! One, two, three, wheee!' with ten ordinary steps between (so you can cover some ground). See Chapter 10 where the full activities are described. These kinds of games naturally provide changes in pace, which keep him engaged and keep him moving in the right direction, at the same time.

» Invent a song that goes with the task. This can be anything and you don't need to be able to sing. Just putting a few words and a rhythm to what you are doing changes how it feels. You create a beginning, middle and ending, which helps him and you feel steadier. For example, 'Bits and pieces, bits and pieces, lying on the ground, lying on the ground, makes the place untidy, makes the place untidy, pick them up, pick them up'. 'We're going to put our shoes on, we're going to put our shoes on, here we go, here we go, we're going to put our shoes on' and so on.

Use diversions

Collect things, play I spy, hide in each doorway, think of some small way of distracting any negative focus while you are still actually moving.

Be competitive

Try something more competitive like racing (although use this with some caution and allow him to win – remember why you are doing this!). Who can get there first? 'I bet you can't beat me to the door.'

Practise when it doesn't matter

If he struggles generally with transitions, then practise in a playful way when it doesn't matter. There are many fun ways of having him follow an adult lead while moving, which will help both of you later when it does matter.

» Try 'Red light, green light'; 'Mother may I'; 'Simon says'; 'What's the time Mr Wolf?'

» Stop and start games of any kind will help him develop more ability to make these shifts.

There are also some changes that are happening inside your body and these transitions can also be difficult. Let's move on to look at this.

Staying within a comfortable level of excitement

Some of the things that parents frequently say are comments such as, 'She can get overexcited and then I can't calm her down', 'I can't play rough and tumble because then he becomes aggressive' and 'Parties are a nightmare because he goes over the top and it takes hours to calm him down.'

Being able to successfully change state, from calm and relaxed to excited and energetic and back again, is something that many children (and some adults) struggle with. Excitement and activity may easily turn to aggression or being out of control, and things can ramp up and up until the situation becomes chaotic. The ability to find ways to calm yourself when you have become excited, and to move from one state to another, develops during the early years as described earlier. This is called regulation. When babies are born, they can't do this for themselves. They have to learn how to regulate gradually through others helping them. There are big differences between individuals with how easy or hard this is to learn.

Not everyone is the same

Some babies are just more sensitive and harder to soothe than others. Others are more active, impulsive and likely to become agitated. We're all different and this is especially true of what happens inside our bodies. How we pick up smells and feel touch, what we like and don't like and how our bodies react to stress and excitement are unique to each person. Also, some of us may have had difficult beginnings (like medical procedures or difficult body experiences like gastric reflux) or may not have had the sensitive care we needed. All of these things affect what is happening inside our bodies and can cause difficulties in how we learn to understand and regulate our bodies. Whatever the cause of the difficulty in regulation, the problem we face as parents is similar.

Do you want to know what you can do to help him learn how to manage these changes in his state better? The answer is practise.

Practise through fun

He can only learn through lots of practise with a trusted and sensitive adult helping him. His body needs to go up and down in state, with someone alongside to help the shift happen in a controlled manner. In time, and over lots of repeats, he will start to recognise what it feels like and gradually become more able to control himself. It doesn't matter how old he is. If he has missed out or is still struggling, he will need actual practice with a supportive person beside him. Trying to explain to him what to do, or asking him to calm down, will not work if he doesn't know how.

Practising through Theraplay is a great way of supporting your child to go up and down in state with you alongside him. For example, an activity with two balloons might start quietly (such as, blowing up both balloons), then become very lively (by hitting the balloons randomly around the room), to then becoming calmer through adding more structure (by seeing if you can keep the balloons up with just the back of your hands or elbows), to then becoming calmer again (by putting both balloons into a large bag and then counting how many times you can toss the bag between both of you). In this way, you have supported the change in his body experience in an adult-led and enjoyable way.

You do of course have to choose your activities carefully and to feel confident that you have ways to bring his state down once you have excited him. What you will find is that there are some activities which may be too exciting, and others that may not interest him enough. As a guide: things that involve concentration, higher levels of structure, less movement and more body contact with the floor tend to be calming. Things that involve unpredictable movement or a lot of movement and are less focused, tend to be alerting and may lead your child to get overexcited. Each activity can be done in many ways, so it is not so much a matter of avoiding bubbles at all costs (because he might become out of control), but of finding ways to do the activity in more or less exciting ways.

Think:

» How often do you start something you thought would be fun but then stop it because it went wrong?

» Do you have ways of shifting the atmosphere and continuing with what you are doing, or do you tend to manage difficulties by changing tack? For instance, many parents change the atmosphere by distraction but find it hard to calm things down or finish things off.

Beginning, middle and end

When you really think about it, you may realise that games often end with an abrupt stop because it's going wrong, or you are expecting it to go wrong any minute. Perhaps you don't even start a game like this.

If this is the case, what does your child learn? He could possibly learn that he is not much fun to be with, that you can't cope with him being energetic, or that if he escalates things, then you will stop. This is probably not what you were hoping for.

Think about patterns and everyday things which have a beginning, a middle and an end. Your day is like this. You get up, do something in the day and then go to bed. When you eat your breakfast it's the same, you get things ready, you eat and then you clear away. There is night and day, and there are times of activity and times of quiet. Daily life, and what goes on inside your body, is full of patterns and rhythms. Even when things are very chaotic or difficult, you usually have a feeling about when it started and when it ended.

Concentrating on having a pattern to small things can be very helpful in supporting children with their regulation. Think of any song, or counting to ten, or ready, steady, go. All of these provide a structure with a beginning and ending and they help create some organisation, which helps us to relax and to know what's coming. The same idea can be created in activities which practise going up in excitement and then down again.

Ideas to try: Going up and down deliberately

» First, watch carefully what your child does. Notice what sorts of things get him excited and what things he does to calm down. These things that he naturally does will give you clues about how to help him. It might not look like he's trying to calm down but complete the checklist below and see what he's doing.

» Start an activity quietly, then deliberately make it more exciting (though not too much!) and then bring the energy level down again. You can do this with a very wide range of everyday activities. It's important that you feel confident to bring the energy down before you take it up too much. If you pick a time when things are going OK to practise, then you will find yourself getting better at finding out what works and what doesn't.

» Use songs and rhythm to help change his state and support his regulation. If he can't listen to what you are saying, then start to sing, chant or tap out a rhythm. It can be amazing how he will naturally join your pace. As we described above, you can deliberately go up and down in speed and volume to help him feel what this is like, with you alongside. You are giving his body some practice. For instance, the song 'Motor boat' starts slowly and gets faster (as you move) and then you 'put on the brakes' and go slowly again.

» Match where he is and take it from there. If your child is very loud and energetic you may find it works best to match his energy level (by being loud and vibrant in the way you try to involve him), then once you have his attention and involvement, you have more chance of shifting the pace to help bring him down.

Regulation checklist: Does this sound like your child?

Here are two checklists. If you can tick a lot of these then your child may have difficulties with regulation and will need help and practice. This first checklist is about children who are hyper-aroused.

✓ He gets irritated easily and can go from fine to angry in an instant.

✓ He wants to move a lot, gets overexcited and can't calm down.

✓ He can go out of control and get aggressive when things are noisy and exciting.

✓ He shows quick and jerky movements and his body is tense.

If this sounds like your child, then he will need help to keep steady and not to become overexcited and out of control. High levels of rhythm and structure will probably be of help. Take care with chaotic games.

This second checklist is about children who are hypo-aroused.

✓ He doesn't notice most things and would prefer just to sit.

✓ He doesn't really know what fun or joy are like.

✓ He often looks dreamy or spaced out.

✓ He shows slow movements and his body is floppy and loose.

If this describes your child, then he will need help to get engaged and to express interest and excitement. Try enticing him in quiet ways and gradually help him have new experiences.

Summing up
Lower your expectations and add support at transition points

Transitions are hard for us all. When you are at any transition point, try to lower your expectations about what is acceptable behaviour and provide more support. For example, when Arun has just come out of school, he dumps his coat at your feet in the school playground or, once home, he drops his coat on the floor rather than hanging it up. It might be reasonable to expect him to do better but this is not the best moment to challenge him. Think about how you would support him if he were half his age and do that! Just for these five minutes. You could sing or chant, 'Coats don't go on the ground, let's pick it up (you physically pick it up), there you go'. You could give Arun a welcome home ritual, like a snack and a few moments of reconnecting time. Then he might be in a better frame of mind to settle and manage higher expectations.

 At transition points, lower your expectations and add support. Ask yourself: how would I support him if he were half his age?

Take the conflict out

With all of the ideas that we have explained above, you will see that your child reaches the end point without feeling as if he has had to follow your orders, because you have made it playful. This takes the potential conflict out of the situation and the fun and support of the activity provides enough support to help him get there.

Older children: It's often harder to think of approaches that might work with an older child. You don't want to patronise him by trying something too childlike but a playful approach, rather than just shouting for him to hurry up, is always worth a try. Unexpected humour can sometimes work, like leaving a note on his pile of clothes saying, 'Please pick me up, I'm lonely down here' or making a deal that you will stop singing once he's at the door! Always remember to avoid picking battles when you have all just got up in the morning or you are trying to manage getting through an immediate transition. At times when you think a playful activity will not work, think about avoiding battles by staying calm in yourself, taking a step back and helping him to succeed by giving him some space or simple options.

But it really winds me up!

One of the things that is really hard in managing transitions is that they usually come about when there is a deadline and this creates a feeling of stress. As parents, we've all faced the stress of having to get our child to school on time, being late to work and needing to get our child to bed. At these times, it's hard to be playful or think of ideas. Try to remember that you will be stressed during a transition just as much as he is. Plan a little extra time for the transitions, get ready and practise! Sing your way through your day, count to ten, crack a joke, give yourself a treat. Concentrate on being extra supportive and competent just until you get to the other side of the transition. Then you can relax.

8

Thinking about
Behavioural Issues

As parents, we will all find ourselves facing behaviour from our child that is difficult to deal with from time to time (or sometimes a lot of the time!). You have tried your usual good ways of helping your child but you can't get the behaviour to stop. There is a lot of different advice about how best to deal with behaviour and it might not seem obvious that a playful approach can be helpful. You might think, 'How could a silly game help with behavioural issues? Surely my child needs discipline and consequences for her behaviour?' Let's think about this.

**Exercise: Think of a current behaviour
that you are finding hard to deal with**
Ask yourself the following questions:

1. What do I think my child's behaviour is about? Why does she do it?

2. When I am dealing with it, what do I want the outcome to be?

3. Have my attempts to influence her worked so far?

4. Once I have dealt with the behaviour, what would I like my relationship with her to be like?

Sometimes you will have some kind of explanation for why you think your child is behaving in a particular way. This could include, 'She must be tired. She wants attention. She's upset.' Sometimes you may feel at a loss to know why she is doing something. Most parents will want to feel that they can have some way to stop the behaviour and that when the situation has been resolved they will still feel OK in their relationship with their child. There may be a period of 'cooling off' between them, but they hope that they will be able to pick up the friendly parts of their relationship once things have settled. For some parents and children, sadly life can feel like a constant battle so that the conflict and management of everyday challenges takes over and there is little of the warmth and fun left.

Why does my child do that and what can I do?

Working out how best to respond to your child's behaviour depends on understanding why she is doing it. This part is really important. The way you make sense of her behaviour really influences what you do next.

Let's take an example: Lulu is rushing wildly around the room, crashing into the furniture. You ask her to stop and she doesn't. The tension is rising and it is hard to think. As her parent, you want to try to stop this behaviour. You are worn out and the situation is chaotic and you feel that Lulu is doing this on purpose. You think, 'She could stop if she decided to. She is just doing it to make me angry.' If that's what you think, then you are likely to respond with frustration and you may try to teach Lulu the right way to behave (for example, by telling her off and putting in a consequence such as, 'I told you not to do that, now go upstairs and no TV'). You may start calmly but this situation often turns into conflict.

If you take this typical route and your child does what you have said, then you may have stopped the behaviour this time, but you could also have an angry child now upstairs while you are feeling agitated downstairs. When this kind of parenting becomes your usual approach then, very often, you can end up feeling as if you are disconnected from your child and living in a battleground of winners and losers each time there's a problem.

How can a Theraplay approach help?

At the heart of the Theraplay approach is the aim to become more connected with your child. This requires that you spend a lot of effort trying to really know her, observing what she likes and doesn't like and working out the sorts of things that annoy her or help her feel calm. You try to 'read' her so that you have a good chance of knowing when things aren't OK for her. When you are then faced with difficult behaviour, you may be able to get an idea of what may be happening beneath the surface. Behaviour is often not what it seems. Then you can use different ideas to suit the particular situation. This is another central Theraplay idea: you adjust your approach depending on what is going to help your child in this particular situation. It's not as simple as playing a hand-clapping game to help your child feel calm. Instead it depends on figuring out what is really going on and thinking of an approach that will support your child.

> We need to understand what any difficult behaviour is about before we can know how to try and deal with it. We do have to deal with it though, somehow or another, because that is part of being a parent.

Let's think about some possible reasons that might underlie Lulu's behaviour in the example given above. She may be:

» angry and upset and it may seem that she is trying to get a response from you.

» feeling unwell.

» tired or overstimulated and jumping around is her way of calming herself or handling it.

» anxious or fearful.

What these possibilities show is how one kind of behaviour can have many different reasons underneath it. What we have to remember about children is that often they cannot fully express themselves using spoken language. She may be too young or stressed so she can't tell you how she is feeling. When you ask what is wrong and she ignores you or says, 'I don't know', this is often the truth; she doesn't know. What she does do is to 'show' you that she is not OK through her body language and behaviour. If you look carefully, you might see that your child is 'not quite herself'. The way this comes out can be confusing. A sad child may become aggressive, an anxious child overactive, etc. Your child may not look obviously sad or anxious.

Exercise: Think for a moment

Remember the last time you were ill or something stressful happened in your family? You might have hoped that your child would be sensitive and less demanding, or show some care and understanding about the situation. What actually happened?

Often, she will be very aware that something is not right and she will try to 'be good' for a little while but she cannot keep it up. When she is anxious (because you are ill for instance), she becomes more demanding rather than less. We could call this 'attention needing' since she needs you more because she is upset or worried. Unfortunately though, her need for you has come just at the moment when you have the least energy to give. This means that her feelings of worry often come out by her becoming more demanding of attention from you. It is not that she is trying to make you feel bad but rather that she needs you to reassure her.

How can we use Theraplay ideas? Let's go back to think of ideas to help Lulu who was jumping around the room. Different Theraplay ideas might be used depending on what you think is underlying her behaviour.

Ideas for helping Lulu

You think Lulu may be angry and upset and seems to be trying to get a response from you

When children seem to be deliberately provocative it matters to them that you notice. If you think she is trying to get a response from you then you probably won't want to get involved because it will feel like giving her attention for something negative (this is what we are all taught). You might decide to ignore her but it will likely make her worse as she will escalate her behaviour to try and get you involved. That's what it seems she wants, attention, good or bad. It can feel like a trap. Whatever you do backfires. So, what are the alternatives?

If you try to use Theraplay ideas straight away with Lulu she may well get angry with you (because she's upset and she is expecting a battle), but you might try diverting her energy by getting involved in something nearby which is interesting and allows her to join you somehow. By being playful and unpredictably avoiding a conflict you might find you can shift the atmosphere. For example, you might say, 'Hey, those cushions have given me an idea (talking to yourself), I'm going to make a den' (you start building a den). Lulu is surprised and stops in her tracks. She may try to draw you into a conflict since this has been the atmosphere; she might say, 'They're my cushions.' If you can keep calm, upbeat and inviting with the new idea, she may drop the provocation and join you with something that is constructive and connected. She now has what she needed, some focused time together with you, and you have found a way to lead her there nonverbally and through play. Now that you have helped her calm, she might be able to relax through play and perhaps tell you what happened that had made her upset. You might be able to talk about the jumping around. The focus is on changing the direction of the atmosphere. Lulu may try to create a conflict and you actively shift things in a different direction through being enticing and surprising in the way you engage.

You think Lulu may be feeling unwell

You might try saying, 'Oh Lulu, I don't think you're feeling quite right. Come over here and get cosy. I'll get you a drink and we could read a story together.' The focus is on nurture.

You think Lulu may be tired or overstimulated and jumping around is her way of handling it

You might think over what has happened today and remember that she has already managed all day at school, that the school routine has changed (which she doesn't cope well with) and she is becoming out of control having held herself together all day. You might decide to focus on trying to help her calm down. You probably won't have much luck just asking her to calm down. But if you get alongside her and match her energy levels, and then support her to calm to a quieter activity, this might work. For instance, you might say, 'My goodness, what a long day you have had, and now you are in a really jumpy mood. Come on, let's see if you can jump over these cushions. I bet you can. One, two, three, jump!' (big jump, lively confident voice, holding her hand). Repeat and gradually bring your voice tone and energy down until you can move to something quieter like crawling. You, as the adult, shift the tone and energy level once you have her attention and cooperation. The focus is on trying to help her regulate by providing structure and pattern to the chaos and gradually bringing her state down so that she is calmer and more in control.

You think Lulu may be anxious or fearful

You might be thinking that something has happened to make Lulu behave in this way, something that has made her feel anxious and out of control? If you think she might be fearful then you would avoid confronting her directly or trying to engage her in a lively diverting activity. Instead you might try to create a calm and safe atmosphere by being quiet and kind but present in the room. You might talk aloud about how you can see that she seems worried about something, and find a soothing activity that allows her, in her own time, to come towards you, 'Oh Lulu, I'm not sure what's going on but you seem really worried about something. I'm going to sit over here and maybe in a while you might feel like coming over to join me' (sit away from Lulu doing a quiet activity). The focus is on calming and soothing while being present. This could include providing a snack and a calming activity such as playing 'Sticker match' – play on your own first.

Note: None of the above involved telling off, punishments or consequences. At the end of the examples given, when the behaviour has calmed, your relationship with Lulu is likely to be stronger and more connected. Rather than sending her away and becoming angry with each other, you have stayed alongside her and helped her to find a way into a different state. In all of these examples, you may well talk with Lulu about the unacceptable behaviour at some stage but it will be done once she is calm and feeling close to you. So, feeling safe, she will be more able to make some kind of sense of what she did.

 It is surprising how often a playful approach can overcome discipline issues.

Obviously not all behavioural issues can be dealt with playfully. If your child is very upset or angry, she will not want to be playful. There are also times when a firm voice and some clear limits will be important. For example, you may need to get her seat belt on and it has to happen now. You can, however, still use some of the principles of staying connected with your child to help you get through the situation. You might be very firm with your child while at the same time accepting her feelings and finding ways to reconnect afterwards. For instance, 'I know you don't want it on and you're annoyed but it won't be for long' (click seat belt on).

I'm not in the mood

A frequent block to being playful or trying to connect with your child is that you, as the parent, are not in the mood. You may be feeling irritated or annoyed with your child. You may be trying to get somewhere or get things done and you haven't got the patience or motivation to play or see things from her perspective.

Look back at question 2 at the start of this chapter, 'What do you want the outcome to be?' Most of us would say, 'We want the behaviour to stop.' If a playful approach might stop the behaviour, then that should be great news. Probably that is not the whole story. If the behaviour stops and it has been done playfully you might not feel satisfied. Your friends might say, 'You are rewarding her for being difficult.' You might think, 'She has been naughty, we did something fun and so she won't have learnt her lesson!' This feeling is very common and is something important to consider. Why do we think it is important for our child to suffer? Why do we assume that this is the only way for her to learn?

 Punishment is the least effective way of influencing our children. Building strong relationships and using warmth, sensitivity and playfulness have deep, long-term positive impacts.

When you put your energy into strengthening your relationship with your child, and find creative ways to get alongside (while also dealing with the behaviour), then it is amazing how many difficult behaviours fall away.

Looking after yourself

Putting energy into the ideas in this book, however, requires you to be feeling all right in yourself and there will be times for all of us when this isn't possible. You may be completely worn out. None of us can be super-parents all the time. It is important to take time for yourself, assuming your child is safe. In Theraplay we talk about building in success for your child, so that she feels good about herself.

The same applies to you as her parent. When things are tough, take a Theraplay approach to yourself! Find small ways that you can feel successful, give yourself plenty of nurture and spend time with people who help you feel special, who you can have fun with and who can provide you with some comfort.

Here are some different situations with Theraplay ideas to try

Bobby is very shy and anxious and does not seem to like playing.

Try finding quiet ways of playing alongside him, which may entice him into joining in, in some small way. If you find activities that are interesting to him, without putting him under pressure, you might find that he begins to watch what you are doing and then slowly starts to feel more comfortable and may move towards you. Things like bubbles, feathers or foil may work well because you can find things to do which do not need him to join in, and he can still enjoy watching – for example, watching bubbles fall, watching you to see how far you can blow a feather from your hand. If you take it slowly and don't rush him, he may relax enough to allow you to sit a bit closer or get him a bit involved. The important thing is not to pressure him as he is likely to withdraw. Make sure you choose very simple games where the game will work just with you doing it.

Sam escalates things very easily. If I start to play with him then he quickly gets out of control and can get aggressive. I don't know how to calm him down and I usually end up shouting at him. So now I avoid playing.

This is a very hard situation when you feel like your attempts to have fun always go wrong. Sam is going to need lots of support from you to help him get more control over his body regulation. Try to practise going up and down in energy in the way you play with Sam. If you know that rough and tumble gets him wound up, so that things go out of control, then look for other more structured ways of doing something physical. For instance, find ways of moving around while you are holding his hands (for example, 'Funny ways to cross the room', starting big and getting smaller, or the other way around). Introduce start and stop activities as often as you can (such as 'Red light, green light') and games that involve rhythm and pattern. An activity that works well is ten jumps on a cushion (with you holding his hand), then a big jump off and start again.

Sam will probably need a lot of structured practice with you supporting him to help him start to gain more control over the changes happening in his body. Of course, you will need to find ways of bringing his energy levels down before you experiment too much with taking him up! It is helpful to notice what sorts of things trigger his aggression. It is common that high movement and unpredictable movement can get children too excited and then they lose control. Things like feathers, bubbles and balloons (flighty things) and things like having a ball (which move fast and unpredictably) may be particularly likely to overexcite Sam. Look for ideas which are more organised and involve concentration or some actual physical effort for Sam (pulling, wheel-barrow, jumping). See Chapter 7 for more ideas.

Keira is very sensitive and gives up easily so that when I try and play it usually goes wrong and she probably ends up feeling worse about herself.

Choose activities which have very low levels of challenge in them so you can be sure that the game can succeed. It can be surprising how easily a sensitive child can feel as though they have failed. The sorts of activities that will go better are those with no competition, those that are easy to get right (even if getting things right is not part of your plan, that may be what Keira is thinking about) and give practical support so that the game works out well whatever Keira does. Ideas like 'La la magnets' (where you hold hands, say 'la, la, la' and then join up some part of your bodies – like elbows, fingers, knees) tend to be good choices. There is a level of structure and predictability in the game which will help Keira relax and it is hard for it to go wrong if you keep it simple. Similarly, 'Beanbag drop' (with you catching the beanbag together), or something which really captures her attention so she stops thinking too much, may work well. Notice the times when Keira genuinely relaxes and ask yourself what it is about the situation that has helped her to do this. Then build these ideas into your game.

Shannon acts cool and as though playing is beneath her. I can't seem to find ways to have fun with her. Not many laughs in our house.

This is typical of many teenagers but can also be the case with quite young children. It is always upsetting for you as the parent when you are trying to engage and have fun with your child and they look at you as if there's something wrong with you! One of the things about the Theraplay approach is that you try to keep an upbeat positive kind of approach even in the face of surliness. The hope is that via some creative persistence you will find a way to draw your child or teen in. This may mean you feel and look rather silly but keep remembering the playful part of your child underneath the veneer of 'cool' and see if you can entice her out. This is one occasion not to respond only to the message she is giving to 'back off'. You will know that if you follow her lead in this way you will just end up separate and disconnected.

It's important in this situation not to take a conde-scending manner or to pick very young activities as this will probably annoy Shannon. Choose ideas with higher levels of challenge in them, something that is actually quite hard (and if possible cool and age appropriate) and start there. For instance, play 'Cotton ball hockey' (blow the ball across a cushion or use straws and a cotton ball) or any game that involves the invitation, 'I bet you can't do this. Come on then, show me what you can do.' This is likely to involve you losing heavily! However, it may get Shannon involved, laughing and more accepting of trying to do something enjoyable together and you can often start this way and move towards something more cooperative. There are many activities which can be made more appealing to a child like Shannon by increasing the level of challenge, and if you think of many adolescent games, they will often use challenge as a way to start playing and then may become less self-conscious in the way they play. Other activities that are particularly appealing are those which are unusual and allow fiddling with a prop, like foil, where Shannon's curiosity may get the better of her.

Summing up

You can see in these last two examples that we suggest very low challenge for Keira but high challenge as a way of drawing Shannon in. This is a key part of the Theraplay approach. Different approaches are needed for different situations. This also happens while you are actually in the middle of playing with your child. One moment they are with you and joining in happily and then next something has happened that has meant they withdraw or become too active. The key is to understand what may be underlying the behaviour.

🖐 Ask yourself: what is it that will help in this moment with my particular child as she is right now?

Theraplay will not help with all difficulties of course, but by looking underneath the difficult behaviour and trying to understand what the behaviour is about, you might see that many behaviours are not really about your child deliberately being 'naughty'. They come about for a wide range of reasons, and finding new ways to redirect, manage and repair using playfulness can make a big difference.

Remember too that Theraplay is not simply a bunch of activities. The activities are very useful but are there only as a vehicle to bring you together. The Theraplay approach is about really noticing and working out what may be going on for your child and adapting what you do, and how you do it, to give you both the best chance of making something good happen. If you can find ways of becoming more connected and working together then many difficult behaviours fall away.

9
Final Thoughts

As you can see, there are many ways of using Theraplay –
in different situations, for different reasons and in different
ways. You might use ideas to help you get your child to
come home from the park or to spend one-to-one time
connecting with your child. You might get ideas about
how to calm your overexcited child or give confidence to
your anxious one. Whatever it is you want to do, here are
some key things to remember.

Theraplay is about:

» *giving hope and increasing joy.* Laughing and playing
without judgement and anxiety is deeply healing.
Small moments of shared joy and delight strengthen
the bond between you and can make hard times
seem more hopeful.

» *connecting and being together.* This is the important part. It's not about doing an activity properly or having something to show for it. The games and props actually don't really matter, it's what they create between the two of you. Because they are tried and tested they are good places to start to get this connection going.

» *really getting to know your child.* Theraplay is all about really getting to know him by carefully watching how he responds and adapting what you are doing. You will get very good at noticing his body signals about when something feels nice or too much and you will get better at working out how to help.

» *showing your child he is special.* Theraplay focuses on the uniqueness of your child, what is special about him and how you notice and appreciate him.

» *being in the 'here and now',* in the present moment with your child. You are trying to focus on what it is you are doing together right now.

» *nonverbal sensory felt experience.* It's not about talking about the past or behaviours but about having a nonverbal experience of being together, which may challenge these things without having to name them. Even if there is a lot going on, having an experience of togetherness which you can both feel in your bodies can really help.

» *helping your child become more regulated.* By watching him carefully and using fun to draw him in, you can help him practise going up and down in energy levels. You can practise beginnings and endings, stopping and starting, following and leading.

» *helping your child relax and be a child.* By relieving him from undue responsibility and being an upbeat and confident leader, you can give him the experience that it feels good to be taken care of, that you will look after him, and that he can just be small.

» *being aware of your child's emotional needs.* He may have different abilities in different areas. Theraplay is about connecting at his emotional age – this is what makes the connection powerful and direct.

» *helping things to go well.* Your role is to find ways of playing that are successful, pitching games at a simple level so that they work out well, and finding ways to repair when things go wrong.

» *finding new ways around difficult behaviours.* You will be surprised how often conflict and difficult behaviours can be avoided, or resolved, through a warm and playful approach.

Questions and answers

We hope that you have found some ideas that you might try within this book. Everyone's situation is unique but there are some common questions that come up when thinking about Theraplay. We will try to answer some of these here.

Some of the activities seem babyish. Is this OK?

We cannot move forward and become independent without the early building blocks of relationships being in place, so sometimes as a parent it can feel as though you are going backwards to move forwards. This is not the same as 'babying' your child. If he has a developmental gap (perhaps he missed out on a stage or needs to go back to something), then he may need to play younger games and this will keep coming up until the gap is filled. You may also find that at times of stress he returns to younger-aged play. That is fine. For instance, having to be 'brave' at school and follow the lesson, the rules and deal with friendships may take all of his resources and he may need to 'fill up' again, being cared for by you, once he gets home.

Using Theraplay, you are trying to find ways of really connecting with him and helping him to relax. Theraplay is designed to appeal to your child at his emotional age rather than his actual age, so, for example, he might be eight but actually enjoy playing more like a four-year-old. This might mean that he gets pleasure from very young games. You might worry that it feels wrong or you might think that young games will not help him grow up and become independent. The important thing is to see what he likes and what he responds to, and go from there. The goal is to deepen your relationship with him. To do this, you need to meet him at his level. Look at what he is drawn to, what toys and TV programmes he likes. What does he do when no one is looking? If you play a young game with him (like Peek-a-boo or Sticky nose with a cotton ball) and he finds it funny, then this may be a sign that he has some developmental gaps that need filling. Don't worry. Try to enjoy his pleasure. In time, he will be less interested in these young games and then you will know you have filled the gaps enough.

Of course, we do need to think about what is appropriate for different ages and make sure we don't embarrass or humiliate our child. All activities can be adapted so that they can meet young needs but be presented in an older manner. Let's look at this next.

How do Theraplay ideas work with older children?

It might look a bit different with your older child or teen but he still needs to feel connected to you, just as much as your younger one does. In fact, there are two main phases in your child's development when he particularly needs to keep coming back to reconnect with you. These are the times when he is moving away from you and exploring the world (he moves away and then needs to come back). This happens most obviously at the toddler and then the teenage stage. When your toddler starts to move and explore, he will frequently come back to check in with you. Then when your child becomes a teenager and he is moving towards more independence, he once again needs to keep checking in with you. You might not obviously think of your teenager as needing you a lot at this time but he does. His behaviour is often very changeable, like a mature person one minute and a toddler the next! He does not seem to need you but then comes rushing back. It is a time of uncertainty and insecurity for him and it's important to remember you are still his safe base. If you can find ways to reconnect playfully with him (rather than through arguments) when he's an older child, then it can make a big difference.

The same Theraplay principles apply in terms of finding genuine, 'here and now' ways of connecting with your older child. How this looks will be more age appropriate. For instance, you might adapt ordinary activities into a nurturing time between you – make efforts to check on a stubbed toe, provide him with a favourite snack or sit with him watching a film. You might try to draw him into playfulness through humour or through choosing activities that have more of a challenge component to them (as these are the things older children will often be interested in). For instance, a game of thumb wrestling, a race or a game of 'Cotton ball blow' (with cotton ball and straw) may get you being playful together. If you look at the games teenagers enjoy with their friends (such as target aiming games, egging each other on to try things, tasting competitions and a wide range of sport), then you will see how wholehearted they can be in their play. It's not that they can't play but more that they may be reluctant to be playful with you! The knack is in trying to find ways to entice him. You can't make him do something he doesn't want to do, so you will need to be surprising, persistent and creative. Once you find ways to have these close times together, many parents say that they are 'amazed by how much he actually wants to be looked after, he seems much younger again, like I've got him back. I didn't realise that I was missing him.'

My child wants to talk about things and a lot is going on. Does that mean I shouldn't use Theraplay?

If your child really wants to talk about something, then it is important to listen and show support. This might be a time to talk rather than play, especially if he is upset or angry and wants to share his experience with you. It doesn't mean you can't use Theraplay ideas as well. You might want to give nurture by providing a cosy place to sit, bringing him a snack or putting an arm around him.

There are also times when children talk as a way of distracting you (and you will do the same). If you are starting to get closer and he is not used to this feeling, then it may make him anxious. He may bring up topics that take away the intense feeling of togetherness. For instance, he may suddenly point at something, change the topic or mention bullying or something that will draw you into a conversation. In this situation, he is using the talking as a way to divert away from the 'here and now' experience, which is understandable because the new closeness feels a bit strange. In this situation, it might be more helpful not to talk but to find ways to get back to a nonverbal way of relating. You may need to find ways to make it less intense so that he is more comfortable (for example, by doing activities which reduce eye contact, playing something side by side or by using a prop, like foil or cotton balls). Gradually he will start to feel more relaxed with this closeness.

Another thing to think about is that children and teenagers often say that it is big relief when adults find ways to be with them without asking questions or talking about the past. We have heard children say, 'I'm tired of going over things, all we can do is talk about the past, behaviours or homework.' We often forget how to play with our children and have fun times with them. Sadly, in our busy lives most of our time with our children can get taken up with managing things rather than really being together. Even very short moments of playful connection can make a difference.

My child has many complex needs. Can I still use Theraplay?

There are many kinds of difficulties which could be seen as complex. Maybe your child has been diagnosed with autism or has sensory processing difficulties. Perhaps your child has experienced significant developmental trauma and finds any 'to and fro' connected relationship difficult. In each situation, the Theraplay approach can be adapted to make it a manageable experience for your child. In a complex situation, Theraplay will unlikely be the answer to all your difficulties but it can add something to your overall parenting approach. You might want to seek specialist support (see the information below).

The most typical adaptations we make for complex difficulties are based on knowing your child well and so, as a parent, you are usually in the best position to know what will work and what won't. Here are some brief examples of adaptations of Theraplay for some common difficulties.

My child struggles with intimacy and nurture.

You may find that you have more luck with activities that are less focused on nurture and initially play that way until he feels a bit more confident that you are not going to do something unpleasant. Remember, to him, touch or intimacy may feel unpleasant. When you begin to introduce more touch, find ways to provide touch and care that are less direct to start off with. For instance, sit side by side rather than opposite (this allows him to avoid looking at you and makes it less demanding). Focus on a prop or include some touch which is a natural part of an activity rather than making a fuss of caring for him (this will probably be too hard for him). The hope is that over time he may start to feel more comfortable with receiving nurture but this does have to be approached carefully – an experience is only nurturing if he experiences it as such (just because he accepts a hug, that doesn't mean it's a positive experience, he may be flinching or tensing his body while he does so). Watching his nonverbal responses is really important, especially if he doesn't communicate easily.

My child might start to cuddle or play and then will suddenly bite me or do something mean.

Notice when he does this. It could be that he is beginning to relax (for example, into a game or a cuddle) and then he suddenly realises what is happening and this makes him feel vulnerable. If you are used to surviving on your own, then having new experiences of intimacy or being connected to another person can be hard. If he 'cuts out' or bites, this may be a sign that the contact was too intense for him. Adapt your approach so that it is less intense but don't stop trying. As the feeling becomes more familiar he may be able to manage more.

My child seems to try to change each activity as soon as it gets going. Playing only lasts a few moments before he moves on to another thing.

If your child is not used to the 'to and fro' of close relating with another person then, to start with, it may feel very uncomfortable. The feeling of closeness and 'being together' doesn't feel familiar or right. For quite some time he may try to change the activity, and keep moving the goalposts, as a way of managing his own anxiety. Being disconnected and on his own is what he is used to so he might do quite a lot to get back to this familiar feeling. Although you might catch his interest for a short time, he will try his hardest to distract you and change the game. Remember, it may take some time before a genuine 'to and fro' kind of relationship feels better to him. Be patient, keep trying and try to resist having an argument or battle with him. This may well be what is more familiar to him but it won't help him to go in this direction. Remember that even five seconds of a genuine, playful interaction is progress. Focus on extending this, little by little.

Where can I find out more information?

The main website about Theraplay is at www.theraplay. org. This is the Theraplay® Institute USA website and has a lot of information about Theraplay resources, training and lists of qualified practitioners. Some other countries have their own Theraplay websites and resources and there are some key books that you may be interested in looking at for more information. This information is available in Chapter 11. All of the activities mentioned in this book are described in Chapter 10.

How can I find a qualified Theraplay practitioner?

There are qualified Theraplay practitioners around the world. If you are looking for specialist help you will want to know that the person you work with is properly qualified and experienced. There are three stages of qualification, which are:

» Foundational Theraplay Practitioner (this is the first stage).

» Intermediate Theraplay Practitioner.

» Certified Theraplay Practitioner (this is the last stage).

We suggest that you find someone who has had supervision with The Theraplay® Institute and is qualified to at least Foundational Theraplay Practitioner.

Before people can start supervision, they have to attend a Level 1 Theraplay Training. They then have to complete a Level 2 Theraplay Training and have more supervision to become fully certified. People who complete Level 1 and 2 trainings can say they are using Theraplay Informed Practice but they may not have had any supervision. We believe that supervision is essential for good practice and suggest that you *find someone who has had supervision and has been endorsed by The Theraplay® Institute by getting a Theraplay Practitioner Certificate.* When seeking help for your family you can often feel vulnerable. None of us wants to admit we have problems we can't sort out on our own and this can make it more difficult to check out the person who is offering help. It is important you feel confident in the person you are working with so, if you are in doubt, trust your instincts and look elsewhere. There are many talented Theraplay practitioners available and taking the brave step of looking for support can make a real difference to family life.

Are there courses for parents?

There are Theraplay courses for parents and for professionals. Level 1 and 2 Theraplay training is aimed at professionals. Some adoptive parents and foster carers do attend these courses if they are also involved in supporting children in a work role. There is also a Group Theraplay training programme which is mainly aimed at schools.

There are separate Theraplay courses for parents. These are presented as an overview day or a series of short workshops to fit in with childcare. All courses are advertised on the www.theraplay.org website. If you can't find what you are looking for, please send a request email to The Theraplay® Institute and someone will help you organise a course.

10

Description of
Theraplay Activities

This chapter lists activities for you to try with your child. The activities are organised here under each dimension: structure, engagement, nurture and challenge. Many of the activities could be included under more than one dimension – for example, hand-clapping games can be both engaging and structuring. To avoid repetition, we have listed each activity once.

Many of the activities involve some kind of touch, whether that is picking up your child, putting on lotion or playing an active game while holding hands. The way you play the games will be unique to you and your child. The thing to remember is that all touch needs to feel safe and kind and be for the benefit of your child. The 'no hurts' rule in Theraplay means no hurts to anyone, including you.

With activities that involve lifting or physically supporting your child, make sure that your child is light enough and you are strong enough to hold her safely; otherwise, adapt the game so that it works for you. When touching your child, try to avoid tickling. Although tickling is often seen as something funny to do, for many of us it can also be unpleasant, especially when you are not in control of when it stops. In general, we find that it is usually better to use a firm, calm and non-tickling touch.

Watch your child carefully so you can see whether she likes the touch or not.

Some activities use items such as lotion, talcum powder and food. You don't have to follow exactly what the activities suggest here. Adapt the activities so that they suit your child. Choose food your child likes and check that she can tolerate substances such as lotion on her skin. It is usually possible to find lotions which fit the needs of particular children (such as hypoallergenic skin lotions), non-sugar food items and alternatives to the different materials suggested here.

The aim of the Theraplay approach is to help you feel more connected with your child, so if a game is going well, try to extend it to keep the feeling going. For instance, you may draw around her hand and think the activity is over, but you could admire what you can see, compare the drawing with her hand, look for lines, check how much bigger your hand is and draw around her other hand. In this way, an activity becomes more than just doing one thing together and it is the experience of being together, rather than the end product (for example, the drawing), that is the important part.

Most of the activities here are for you and your child to do as a pair. Many can be easily adapted for more than two people and can also be adapted if you have mobility difficulties. Feel free to be creative and make up your own versions. We haven't said what age each activity is for because children are all different and you will know best which games to try.

The Theraplay® Institute publishes books and resources with additional activities in them – see Chapter 11 for more details.

Structure activities

A quick word about signals: Using signals to indicate when to start will add structure to any activity. Start with simple signals, such as 'One, two, three, go' or 'Ready, set, go.' You can then use more complicated signals, such as listening for a selected word in a series, or watching for a visual signal, such as a wink or other facial movement. Don't use signals in every activity because they can slow down the pace or can take away the playful, light-hearted tone that you want to create.

Beanbag drop

Place a beanbag or soft toy on your own head and put your hands under your child's outstretched hands at waist level. Then give a signal (such as, 'ready, steady, drop') and drop the beanbag into your child's hands by tilting your head toward your child. Take turns.

If your child cannot catch very well, then put her hands in yours and bring all your four hands together to catch the beanbag. You could open your hands to let the beanbag fall through to the ground. You can also play this game sitting on the floor.

Blanket run

This involves two parents and your child. Your child sits on one parent's lap facing the other parent with a small blanket lying on the floor between them. On a signal, both parents lift the blanket and your child runs or crawls under the blanket into the arms of the other parent.

Cotton ball blow

You and your child hold a scarf or long piece of cloth between you. You place a cotton wool ball at one end of the scarf and blow it back and forth to your child.

Alternatives can include you placing the cotton ball in your cupped hands and then blowing it into your child's hands. Or you could fold up the long sides of a piece of tin foil (as long as your child's arm or leg,) and blow the cotton ball back and forth on the foil tray. Or you could both lie on your tummies and blow the cotton ball back and forth between you on the floor.

Drawing around hands, feet or bodies

Make a picture of your child's hand or foot by drawing around it on a piece of paper. You can move on to drawing around her whole body, but check your child's reaction to this. Drawing around her whole body requires your child to lie still for some time and this can be challenging. So, you might want to build up to this by doing small body parts at first (like just a hand). Watch your child to make sure that she is feeling OK. It's helpful to talk to your child whilst doing this so she knows what you are doing – for example, saying, 'I'm coming to your ankle, I'm coming to the tickle spot under your arm. I am going to try and do this without tickling you.'

Eye signals

Hold hands with your child and stand facing each other. You use eye signals to indicate the direction and number of steps to take – for example, when you wink your left eye two times, both you and your child take two side steps to your left. If winking is difficult, then instead tilt your head or purse your lips to the left and right. Move around the room like this. To make it more challenging, you can add signals for forward and backward movement as well (moving your head back for backward, head forward for forward). You can also do this while holding a balloon or a pillow between you, by leaning close to each other as you move.

Fish and chips

Say 'fish' and have your child say 'chips' in just the same way. You repeat 'fish' five to ten times while varying the loudness and style of your voice. Your child copies each time and says 'chips'. You can choose any words for this game.

Follow the leader

You stand in front of your child, with your back to her, and she holds on to your waist. You then move in a particular way and your child copies. You can also do this sitting down, moving only arms, head and shoulders.

Funny ways to cross the room

You and your child stand at one end of a room, mat or play space. You tell your child that you are both going to cross the room in a certain way – for example, hopping, tiptoeing, crawling, or walking backward. You can add in funny walks such as a crab walk, elephant walk or scooting.

Hand-stack

Put your hand palm down in front of your child. Have your child put her hand on top of your hand. You then alternate hands to make a stack. Take turns moving the hand from the bottom to the top. You can also move from top to bottom. This can be made more complicated by moving fast or going in slow motion.

Variations include putting lotion on your hands first so that you make a slippery stack. This adds an element of nurture. You can also try stacking feet, forearms, folded arms and fingers. If your child is wary of touch, you can stack hands with one to two inches of space between each hand or finger. For very young children keep your hands stacked on the ground all the way through.

Hokey cokey

You and your child stand opposite each other and sing, 'You put your right foot in. Your right foot out. In out, in out and shake it all about. You do the hokey cokey and you turn around. That's what it's all about. Oh, the hokey cokey!' While singing, you both move your feet, arms and whole bodies into the space between you, and shake them. When you do the 'Hokey cokey', you dance in whatever way you like, arms in air, with playful, energetic gestures.

Jump into my arms

Have your child stand on pillows or the sofa. You then give a signal, such as, 'One, two, three, jump!' for your child to jump into your arms.

La la magnets

You and your child hold hands with each other while sitting or standing opposite each other. You both swing your hands from side to side while you say, 'La, la, la'. You then say a part of the body that will be stuck together like magnets. For example, 'La, la, la, elbows' and you each put your elbows together as if they are stuck together like magnets. Then you both hold hands again and say 'La, la, la' and say a different body part such as 'knees'. You and your child put your knees together. You repeat this sequence saying a different body part each time.

Measuring

Measure your child's height, length of arms, legs, feet, hands, and so on. You can keep a record of this for later comparisons. You can use a measuring tape, wool or ribbon. Measure surprising things, such as your child's smile, the length of her ears, the circumference of her head, or even how high she can jump. You can use fruit leather for measuring, then tear off the length and feed it to your child. This will mix structure with nurture.

Mirroring

Face your child and then move your arms, face or other body parts and ask your child to move in the same way. If your child is very active, you could use slow motion and vary the speed. You and your child could take turns being the leader.

Mother, may I?

You give instructions to your child to do something – for example, 'Take three giant steps toward me.' Your child has to say, 'Mother, may I?' before responding to the command. If the child forgets, she must return to the starting line. The goal is to have your child come to you and get a hug on arrival.

Motor boat

Holding hands with your child, walk around the room, chanting 'Motor boat, motor boat, go so slow. Motor boat, motor boat, go so fast. Motor boat, motor boat, step on the gas!' You gradually increase the speed until it is very fast. Suddenly you say, 'Put on the brakes!' and stop. You then start over with the slow tempo.

Patty-cake

Hold your child's hands and lead her through the song and handclap. Sing or say, 'Patty-cake, patty-cake, baker's man. Bake me a cake as fast as you can. Roll it and pat it and mark it with a [your child's initial]. And toss it in the oven for [child's name] and me!' You can vary this by using your feet.

Play dough squeeze or prints

Place a ball of play dough between your child's hands. Then place your hands on the outside of your child's hands and, while looking directly in her eyes, say 'Squeeeeeeze!' while you firmly press your hands and hers into the dough. You can also use play dough to make finger-, hand- and footprints.

Pop the bubble

Blow a soap bubble and catch it on the wand. Playfully tell your child to pop the bubble with a particular body part – for example, her finger, toe, elbow, shoulder or ear. This is a structured way of playing with bubbles.

You can also blow lots of bubbles into the air and playfully tell your child to pop them all with a particular body part, such as hands, elbows or a handclap. You can vary the speed of this game by, for example, having your child pop all the bubbles as quickly as she can. You could add in a signal so your child knows when to pop.

Red light, green light

Ask your child to do something, such as run, jump, move arms. Green light means go, red light means stop.

Ring-a-ring-a-roses

Hold hands and walk around in a circle chanting, 'Ring-a-ring-a-roses. A pocketful of posies. Attishoo, attishoo, we all fall down.' You walk round in a circle while singing and then you both fall down at the end.

Simon says

This is similar to 'Mother, may I?' but with the added challenge that your child must watch out for commands that do not have 'Simon says' in the phrase. When the game is underway, you can suddenly not say 'Simon says', and your child may do the action without thinking. You can take it in terms to be the leader.

Three-legged walk
Stand beside your child. Tie your two adjacent legs together with a scarf or ribbon. With arms around each other's waist, you both walk across the room. Your job is to coordinate the movement. For example, you can say 'inside, outside' to indicate which foot to use. You can add obstacles (such as pillows, chairs) to make this more challenging.

Toilet-paper-bust-out
Wrap your child's legs, arms, or whole body with toilet paper, paper towels or crepe paper. If your child is hesitant, then let her know what is going to happen by having her hold her hands in front of her body and wrap them first. On a signal, have your child break out of the wrapping.

What's the time Mr Wolf?
You stand on one side of the room and your child stands on the other, facing each other. Your child calls out, 'What's the time Mr Wolf?' You reply, 'One o'clock' and your child takes one step towards you. You can vary the time you give to vary the number of steps your child takes towards you. Once she gets to you, you can give her a big hug. You can also add in a reply of 'lunchtime' and you then playfully catch her and give her a hug.

Engagement
Beep and honk
Press your child's nose and say 'Beep!' then press her chin and say 'Honk!' Guide your child to touch your nose

and chin. Make appropriate beeps and honks, as you are touched.

As a variation of this activity, you can make a special noise when you touch a specific face or body part, for example, elephant trumpeting when you touch a knee. Try to remember which noise goes with the part when you do a series of touches.

Blow me over
Sit facing your child and, while holding her hands (you can cradle a younger child in your lap), have your child 'blow you over'. You fall back as your child blows. Once your child understands the game, you can blow her over.

Check-ups
Check your child's body parts, such as her nose, chin, ears, cheeks, fingers, toes, knees to see if they are warm or cold, hard or soft, wiggly or quiet, and so on. Count her freckles, toes, fingers and knuckles. Check her strong muscles and high jumps.

Copy funny faces
Stand or sit facing your child. You pull a funny face and your child copies it.

Counting fingers and knuckles
Count your child's fingers from one to five on one hand and then, starting with ten on the other hand, count down to six. Say with a puzzled look, 'Five and six make eleven. Do you have eleven fingers?' Your older child will enjoy the joke. Your younger child won't get it.

You can also count all the knuckles on both of her hands. Your child may be surprised to learn that she has 28 knuckles.

Create a special handshake

Make up a special handshake with your child, taking turns to add new gestures – for example, high-five, clasp hands, wiggle fingers, and so on.

Creating rhythms with cups

You and your child sit opposite each other, or side by side, at a table. You each hold an upturned paper cup in each hand so that the top of each cup is on the table. You make up a rhythm by tapping the cups in sequences.

Foil prints

Shape a piece of aluminium tin foil around your child's elbow, hand, foot, face, ear, or other body part. It helps to place a pillow under the foil and have your child press her hand or foot into the soft surface to get impressions of her fingers and toes. This is also a structuring activity since it defines body shapes and boundaries.

Fortune telling

Take your child's hand in yours and pretend to read her fortune by looking at her palm. Say lots of positive things about her and her future.

Handclapping games

You might know a few chants such as, 'Miss Mary Mack' or 'A sailor went to sea.' A search on the Internet will find many of these. You can vary the complexity of the rhythmic pattern and the chant, depending on your child's ability. Always make sure that you start by doing the clapping pattern slowly so that you can easily get into a pattern once you add the rhyme.

Hello, goodbye

Your child sits in your lap so you are face-to-face. You support your child's back with your hands and say, 'Hello' and then dip your child backwards while saying 'Goodbye.' You then bring your child back up and say, 'Hello.'

This can be done standing, with your child's legs around your waist (if your child is young and light to hold).

Knock on the door

This is a simple baby activity and there many variations across the world. You sing, 'Knock on the door' (and tap on your child's forehead), 'Peep in' (you peek into your child's eyes), 'Lift up the latch' (you gently push up your child's nose) and 'Walk in!' (you pretend to walk your fingers into your child's open mouth or pop a piece of food in).

Make up a rap

You and your child make up sentences and chant them like a rap. For example, 'I am a mum and this is my son, we're finding some ways to have some fun, take it high and take it low, make it fast and make it slow!'

Peek-a-boo

Hold your child's hands (or feet) together in front of your face. Peek around or separate the hands (or feet) to 'find' your child.

A lovely variation is to use a sheer scarf to hide your face or your child's, and then pull it off to discover each other.

Piggy-back/Horsey-back ride

Help your child get onto your back. Jog around the room with your child on your back. Your child can give signals such as, "Whoa!' and 'Giddy-up!' The strength of your back determines how old or heavy your child can be for this game.

Pop cheeks
Inflate your cheeks with air and help your child to pop them with his hands or feet. Your child then inflates her cheeks and you pop them in turn.

Popcorn toes
While you take your child's shoes off, ask if she has popcorn, peanuts, grapes and so forth, inside her shoe. Then take her shoe off and discover her wonderful toes.

Push-me-over, land-on-my-knees
Kneel in front of your standing child (so that your child comes to your eye level) or sit in front of your sitting child. Hold your child's hands. On a signal, have your child push you. As you fall back, pull your child onto your knees and 'fly' your child smoothly or bounce her up and down.

Push-me-over, pull-me-up
Sit on the floor in front of your child. Place your child's palms against yours, or put your child's feet against your shoulders. On a signal, have your child push you over. You fall back in an exaggerated way. Then, stretch out your hands so that your child can pull you back up.

Row, row, row your boat
Sing the familiar song, adding your child's name at the end ('Lara's such a dream'). If your child is small, she can be held in your lap. If older, she can sit facing you. By clasping her forearms rather than her hands, she will feel more secure and connected.

You can vary the tempo from fast to slow and back again to practise regulation. You can also rock from side to side. The second, more exciting verse ends with 'If you see a crocodile, don't forget to scream.' You can scream loudly at that point.

Sticker match

Put a colourful sticker on your child and have her put stickers on you in the same place. Carry on until you are both decorated in the same way. After the stickers are applied, you and your child can touch matching stickers together – for example, nose to nose, elbow to elbow – before removing them.

Sticky nose

Put a colourful sticker on your own nose. Ask your child to take it off. As an alternative, you can stick a cotton ball on your nose with lotion. Then, have your child blow it off.

This is the way the baby rides

You hold your child on your lap and bounce her, varying the pace as she moves from baby, to lady, to gentleman, to farmer. Another version of this activity is 'Trot, trot to Boston, Trot, trot to Lynn, Trot, trot to Boston, All fall in!' Let your child gently 'fall' off your lap at the end.

This little pig went to market

Wiggle each toe as you chant, 'This little pig went to market. This little pig stayed home. This little pig had roast beef. This little pig had none. This little pig cried "Wee, wee, wee," all the way home.' You can change the details to fit your child – for example, 'This little pig likes pizza.'

As you say 'all the way home,' walk your fingers up your child's arm in a playful way rather than tickling her tummy.

It's usually better to use firm pressure and a calm approach instead of tickling.

Wiggle toes

Feel for wiggle toes through your child's shoes or socks as part of a greeting and check-up. You can remove your child's shoes or socks to discover her toes.

Nurture

Blanket swing

This involves two parents and your child. Spread a blanket on the floor and have your child lie down in the middle. You both gather up the corners of the blanket and give a gentle swing while singing a song. At the end bring her down for a 'soft landing'.

Position yourselves so that one of you can see your child's face. If your child is fearful of being lifted off the floor, let her remain in contact with the floor as you gently rotate the blanket around in a circle.

Caring for hurts

Notice and care for scratches, bruises, hurts, 'ouchies' or 'poorlies'. Put lotion on or around the hurt, touch with a cotton ball or blow a kiss. You don't need to announce, 'Let's see how many hurts you have.'

Cotton ball or feather guess

First demonstrate by touching your child's hand with a cotton ball and a feather; ask her to notice the difference between the two sensations. Then have your child close her eyes and tell you where you have touched her and whether you did it with a cotton ball or a feather. This adds challenge to a nurturing activity. If your child is not comfortable closing her eyes, have her look away.

Cotton ball soothe
Have your child relax on pillows or in your arms. You gently stroke your child's face, arms or hands with a cotton ball. You can quietly describe the features that you are outlining: rosy cheeks, smiling mouth, upturned nose.

Cotton ball touch
First, have your child hold out her hand while you do a gentle touch on one of her fingers. Have her point to or tell you which finger you touched. Then have your child close her eyes (or turn her head to one side if closing eyes bothers her). Touch her gently with a cotton ball. Have her open her eyes and indicate where you touched her.

Decorate child
Make rings, necklaces, bracelets with play dough, soapy foam, crepe paper streamers or aluminium foil.

Doughnut or pretzel challenge
Put a doughnut or pretzel on your finger. See how many bites your child can take before breaking the circle.

Face painting
Paint flowers and hearts on cheeks or make up your child like a princess or a prince. If your child is a boy, he might find moustaches and beards interesting.

A variation on this is to use a soft dry brush and pretend to paint your child's face, while describing her wonderful cheeks, lovely eyebrows, etc. as you gently brush each part.

Fanning

After a vigorous activity, fan your child with a large pillow, a fan or newspaper. Watch how her hair blows.

Feather match

Prepare two sets of five feathers; if they are coloured, have the sets match. Then decorate your child with one feather (in her hair, tucked into a sleeve, between her fingers). Your child then places a feather on you in the same place. You carry on with a second feather, and so on. You can then admire each other.

Feeding

Cradle your child in your arms while feeding her yoghurt, pudding or juice.

An alternative is to sit your child on your lap or sit facing her. Feed her, listening for crunches and noticing whether she likes the snack and when she is ready for more. You can add variety by having two or three kinds of snack – raisins, nuts, crackers. Have your child close her eyes and guess which snack it is.

If your child refuses to let you feed her at first, allow her to feed herself but make yourself a part of the activity – for example, by commenting on how long she chews, how loud her chews are or what you notice about her that lets you know she likes the food.

Handprints

Rub some finger paint onto your child's hand (or foot). You could use one colour or create a pattern with several colours. It is best to do one hand or foot at a time. Press the painted hand or foot onto paper to make a print. After the prints are made, gently wash, dry and powder her hand or foot.

Lotion or powder prints
Apply lotion or talcum powder to your child's hand or foot and make a print on paper, a floor mat, a pillow, your dark clothing or on a mirror. If you make a lotion print on dark construction paper, you can shake powder on it and then blow or shake it off to enhance the picture (take care to keep the powder away from your child's face). You can also make a pile of powder on a piece of paper and have your child rub her hand or foot in it to make the print.

Lotioning or powdering
Put lotion or talcum powder on your child's arms, hands, legs or feet. You can sing a personalised song as you do this such as, 'Oh lotion, oh lotion on Aisha's feet. It feels so good, it feels so sweet. Oh lotion, oh lotion on Aisha's hands. It feels so good, it feels so grand.' Attend to your child's sensory needs by using firm pressure, or you could use powder, rather than lotion, if your child is sensitive to touch.

Lullaby
Cradle your child in your arms in such a way that you can look into her eyes. Sing your favourite lullaby or any quiet, soothing song. You can add details about your child to the traditional words.

Manicure or pedicure
Soak your child's feet or hands in warm water. Using lotion, massage her feet or hands. Paint your child's toes or fingernails using a variety of colours or letting her choose the colour she wants.

Pizza massage

Have your child lie on blankets and/or pillows on her tummy. Knead her back while describing how delicious the pizza is going to be. Make firm massage movements as if you are kneading the dough. Then use smooth movements as if you are patting out the dough into a pizza base. Use smooth movements to spread the tomato sauce. Then make firm presses whilst you place toppings (cheese, ham, pineapple) onto the pizza.

To vary this, you can make different things, such as tacos, hot dogs or biscuit dough.

Powder palm

Sprinkle some talcum powder onto your child's palm and partially rub it in so that the lines on her palm stand out. Notice shapes and letters. You can then do the same with your palm. Look for differences and similarities between your child's hand and yours.

Powder trail

Place a small pile of talcum powder on newspaper on the floor. Have your child put her feet into the powder so that they are liberally covered with powder. Have her walk on a dark mat or paper leaving footprints as she goes.

Shoe and sock race

Put kisses on your child's feet and put her socks and shoes on before the kiss flies away. You could add new kisses when she goes to bed at night.

Slippery, slippery, slip

This is a lotioning activity with an added element of surprise (it also gives an opportunity to apply firm pressure to your child's body). First rub lotion onto your child's arm or leg. Then while holding firmly well up her arm or leg, say, 'slippery, slippery, slip' and pull towards you, and fall backwards with an exaggerated motion as the slippery arm or leg escapes.

A variation is to see how quickly your child can pull her hand out from between your two slippery hands and squeeze it back into your clasped hands.

Soft and floppy

Have your child lie on the floor and help her get 'all soft and floppy'. Gently jiggle each arm and leg and let it flop to the floor. If your child has difficulty getting floppy, have her get 'stiff like a board' and then let go to be 'soft like a noodle'. Once your child is relaxed, ask her to wiggle just one part of her body: her tummy, her tongue, her big toe, and so forth.

Special kisses

Butterfly kiss: You place your cheek against your child's cheek and flutter your eyelashes so that your child feels the brush of your eyelashes.

Elephant kiss: Hold both fists in front of your mouth (like a pretend trumpet) and keep one fist by your mouth as you make a kissing noise. Move the other fist towards your child's cheek, completing the kissing noise with a flourish as you touch her cheek.

Eskimo kiss: You and your child rub noses.

Temporary tattoos

Apply tattoos or, using washable body paints, draw designs on your child's arms, face or hands.

Trace messages

Using your finger, trace shapes or simple positive messages on your child's back for her to decipher.

Twinkle song

Adapt the words of 'Twinkle, twinkle, little star' to the special characteristics of your child, such as, 'What a special boy you are. Dark brown hair, and soft, soft cheeks. Bright brown eyes from which you peek. Twinkle, twinkle little star. What a special boy you are.' Touch the parts you refer to as you sing to him.

Weather report

Sit with your child sitting in front of you so that you can put your hands on her back. You then describe the weather and rub her back to match the weather. For example, 'It's a warm sunny day', you make a large warm circle. 'The wind is beginning to blow', you swoop your hands lightly across her back making a swishing noise. For 'thunder', use the sides of your hands to pound gently on her back. For 'rain', make light finger taps. For 'lightning', make a big zig zag across her back.

Challenge

Balance on pillows, jump off

Help your child balance on pillows, starting with one and adding more for as long as she can easily manage it. While your child is gaining her balance, hold her around the rib cage, rather than holding her hands. This steadies her and reduces her urge to jump up and down. Once your child is balanced, you can remove your hands and let her experience the feeling of balancing on her own. Then say

'Jump into my arms (or down to the floor) when I give the signal.'

Balancing activities

Your child lies on her back on the floor with her feet up in air. Place one pillow on her feet and help her balance it. Add additional pillows one at a time for as long as she is successful.

Variations include balancing books, beanbags, pillows or hats on your child's head and have her walk across the room.

Balloon balance

Hold a balloon between you and your child (for example, between foreheads, shoulders, elbows or hips) and move across the room without dropping or popping the balloon. See if you can do this without using hands.

Balloon tennis

Keep a balloon in the air using specified body parts – for example, heads, hands, no hands, shoulders. If you choose feet, you both lie on the floor and keep the balloon in the air by kicking it gently. To create more structure and focus, choose a goal for how long you can keep it in the air – for example, 'Let's see if we can count to 20.'

Bubble tennis

Blow soap bubbles high in the air between you and your child. Choose one bubble and blow it back and forth between you until it pops.

Cotton ball hockey or football

You and your child lie on the floor on your tummies (or you could both sit with a pillow between you). You then blow cotton balls back and forth trying to get the cotton ball under your partner's arms or off the edge of the pillow. You can make this a more cooperative game by both blowing hard enough to keep the ball in the middle. You can make it less competitive while increasing challenge by saying how many blows can be used to get the ball across the pillow. You'll find that one blow is easy but two or three are harder to control.

Cooperative cotton ball race
You and your child get on your hands and knees at one end of the room. Take turns to blow a cotton ball (or a ping-pong ball) to the other side of the room. You can try to do it faster and beat your time on repeated trials.

A competitive version would be for you both to have your own cotton ball and see who can get it across the room first.

Cooperative races
There are many ways to organise a cooperative race – for example, taking turns blowing ping-pong balls across the room or kicking balloons. You can time yourselves to see how quickly a goal can be reached.

Crawling race
You and your child crawl on your knees as fast as you can around a stack of pillows. Try to catch each other's feet. Then switch direction.

Feather blow
You and your child each hold a small pillow in front of you. Blow a feather from your pillow towards your child's pillow. She must catch it on her pillow and blow it back.

Feather grab

You blow a feather so your child can grab it.

Jump-start-stop

Have your child walk around the room when you say 'start'. When you say 'stop' she stops. She jumps when you say 'jump'. You can add in more challenge by telling her how far, or how high, she should jump.

Karate chop

Hold a length of toilet paper or paper streamer in front of your child and have her chop it in half when you give a signal.

Magic carpet ride

Have your child sit on a large pillow or small blanket, holding firmly onto the edge. When your child looks at you, pull her around the room. When she breaks eye contact, stop. This works well on a slippery surface, such as a wood or vinyl floor.

Measuring

Measure your child's height against a wall and mark it in some way, then measure when she stands on tiptoes and when she jumps up and touches the wall as high as possible. You can also measure various lengths of jumps or leaps across the floor.

Newspaper punch, Basket toss

Stretch a single sheet of newspaper tightly in front of your child. Have your child punch through the sheet when you give the signal. You must hold the newspaper so firmly that it makes a satisfying pop when your child punches it.

Make sure that you hold the paper so that the punch does not hit you.

You can extend this activity by adding a second or third sheet of paper. You can vary the activity by having your child use the other hand. You can vary the signals you use.

For the Newspaper flick, your child flicks the paper that you are holding so that it makes a satisfying sound.

For the Basket toss, you crush the torn newspaper into balls and then toss them into the bin, or through your arms (by holding them like a basketball hoop).

Partner pull-up

Sit on the floor with your child so that you are holding hands and facing each other with your toes together. On a signal, pull up together to a standing position.

A variation is to sit back to back with your arms interlocked. On a signal, you both push up to a standing position. These activities work best when you are both close in size.

Pick up cotton balls or other small objects with your toes

Start with one or two cotton balls and increase the number. Once the cotton balls have been picked up, you can add throwing them across the room. You can make this more challenging by having your child hop around the room with the cotton ball between her toes.

Pillow push

Place a large pillow between you and your child. Have her push against the pillow to try and push you over.

Seed spitting contest
Feed your child chunks of watermelon or orange or tangerine with seeds. You should eat some too. Both of you save your seeds. Then have your child spit a seed as far as she can. Try to spit your seed as close to hers as possible. You can use other small, edible objects such as beans or small sweets.

Shoe and sock race
You and your child race to see who can put on their shoes and socks, or take them off, first.

Straight face challenge
Your child has to keep a straight face while you try to make her laugh, either by gently touching her (avoid sensitive spots or prolonged tickling) or by making funny faces.

Thumb, arm or leg wrestling
You guide the activity, giving starting signals and keeping it safe.

Tug-of-war
You and your child each hold onto the ends of a scarf, a blanket or a soft rope. Then you each try to pull each other over to your side. Make sure that your child has a good grip and that there is nothing she can bump into. Make it feel exciting by shows of strenuous effort. Let her win. You can also do this with more than two people.

Tunnels
Your child crawls through a tunnel made of pillows and you meet her at the end.

Wheelbarrow
Have your child put her hands on the floor. Stand behind her and clasp her firmly by the ankles or just above the knees. Your child 'walks' on her hands. This is hard work for your child so you should stop as soon as it becomes too tiring.

Wiggle in and out of arms
Your child wiggles out of your encircling arms. She can then wiggle back into your arms. This is usually better if your child is small.

11
Further Resources

You may be interested in finding out more about Theraplay and about some of the approaches we have talked about in this book. As you can imagine, the ideas in this book come from many different sources: books, training and discussion with colleagues as well as our experience of working with many families and having our own children. We are very grateful to all of the people who have helped us with our thinking. We have decided that it wouldn't be helpful to list all their books here as too much information can be off-putting. We know what it's like to buy a book and give up after two pages! Our aim in writing this book about Theraplay has been to find a way to summarise the key ideas in a way which is practical and that busy parents will be able to use. We will therefore suggest just a few books here and you can find further recommendations from there if you want to.

Books about...
Theraplay
The Theraplay® Institute www.theraplay.org sells a few different books and resources like 'flip books' of different activities:

> » *Parenting the Theraplay Way: 214 Engaging, Fun Activities to Create Joyful Connectedness*

> » *Theraplay Activities Flip Book*

There is also a short free video and a lot of information on their website. The Theraplay® Institute books can be bought from their website or from different organisations within your country.

The core Theraplay text (this is a large book which has a lot of detailed information about Theraplay and how Theraplay is used with different kinds of issues) is available from book outlets:

> » *Theraplay: Helping Parents and Children Build Better Relationships through Attachment-Based Play* (3rd edition) (2010) by Phyllis Booth and Ann Jernberg.

Regulation

A good book which summarises sensory development and regulation is *Improving Sensory Processing in Traumatized Children* (2016) by Sarah Lloyd.

Therapeutic parenting

There are many useful books about therapeutic parenting. The parenting approach that fits most closely with Theraplay is that based on the work of Dan Hughes. Here are two books that summarise his approach. They mainly focus on children who have experienced trauma but the approach can usefully apply to all children.

> » *Creating Loving Attachments: Parenting with PACE to Nurture Confidence and Security in the Troubled Child* (2012) by Daniel Hughes and Kim Golding.

» *Everyday Parenting with Security and Love: Using PACE to Provide Foundations for Attachment* (2017) by Kim Golding.

Understanding trauma and the brain

This book would be useful if your child is hypersensitive to signs of danger and finds it hard to trust. The book talks about trauma and explains how your child's brain is working and how attachment-focused therapy can help: *The Neurobiology of Attachment-Focused Therapy: Enhancing Connection and Trust in the Treatment of Children and Adolescents* (2016) by Jon Baylin and Dan Hughes.

Index